D0054940

GOD!

IF YOU ARE REALLY GOD...

ASK AND RECEIVE

BY

L. ALLAN EUBANK

God! If You Are Really God ... is the first in a series of three books to be published about our lives and experiences in Thailand over the period of 42 years.

Other books to be published soon:
On Elephant-backs and Eagle's Wings
Dance-Drama before the Throne: A Thai Experience
God If You Are Really God . . . (in Thai)

Previous publication: **We Are Ambassadors** **(in Thai)**
Suriyaban Press, Bangkok. 1975

"Scripture taken from the HOLY BIBLE, NEW INTERNATIONAL VERSION. Copyright 1973, 1978, 1984 International Bible Society. Used by permission of Zondervan Bible Publishers."

Copyright 2003 by L. Allan Eubank
First printing May 2003, 2nd - August 2003, 3Rd - October 2003

All rights are reserved, but permission is granted to reproduce portions of this book in teaching and ministry if credit is given.

Published by: **TCF Press, P.O. Box 14, Mae Jo,**
Chiang Mai 50290, Thailand

Books may be ordered from TCF Press above or:
THAI CHRISTIAN FOUNDATION
6116 N. Central Expressway Suite 518, L.B. 45
Dallas, TX 75206
E-mail: tjm@McNamaraCo.com

A donation of $10.00 is requested per book. All proceeds go to the Christian Communications Institute, Chiang Mai, Thailand. Add $2 handling and shipping for orders of less than 5 books.

ISBN: 974-85445-3-2

Cover: Photo of central Thailand mountains near Nakorn Sawan (City of Heaven) by A. Schulenburg with author's hands superimposed

Printed by: ACTS Co., Ltd., Chiang Mai, Thailand

DEDICATION

To the Glory of God and with deep gratitude to all of our prayer partners worldwide. They have loved, prayed for and given faithfully to the work here in Thailand. Without them, all that follows would not have been possible.

To my wife, Joan, and our four wonderful children, David, Ruthanne, Laurie and Suewannee. Their loving, patient, and encouraging support during these years has been my inspiration through all the ups and downs of private and public life.

While our children knew many of the people mentioned in this book, they did not know the details of their experiences with God. I trust the reading of these pages will give them a better understanding of their parents' work, and that they will be inspired by the testimonies as we have been.

ACKNOWLEDGMENTS

Grateful tribute must be paid to:

My parents, for their lives of love, faith, loyalty, integrity, service and hard work. Their Christian nurture shaped my life.

My wife, Joan, for her encouragement and her constructive comments and corrections.

My son, David, for his excellent critical insight and positive suggestions in both content and style.

My sister, Margaret, and her husband, Dick Gregory, for their generous hospitality, wise counsel and constructive comments.

The Division of Overseas Ministries, of The Christian Church (Disciples of Christ). They supported our family administratively, educationally, financially, personally, and prayerfully, for 39 years. These experiences are the fruit of their support during these years.

My many excellent professors at Brite Divinity School, Texas Christian University; Yale Divinity School, Yale University; Dallas Theological Seminary; and Perkins School of Theology, Southern Methodist University. Their wisdom helped me to begin to understand the diversity of theological thought and to be thankful that we are finally saved by grace through faith in Jesus Christ not because we fully understand everything.

The Thai Christian Foundation Board for making this book possible, and their support of CCI since its inception. I especially appreciate the early members: George and Mary Ellen Cunyus, James (Bud) and Patsy Porter, Billy and Millie Barrett, Grover and Mary Kay Ellisor, Herbert Hale, Ted Pitzer, Charles Storey, Phyliss Porter Jones, Don and Barbara Jarvis, Dick and Mary Ellen Kelly, Phil and Martiel Orr and E. C. and Mary Louise Rowand. K. Hosek must also be credited for her "above and beyond" service in correspondence and bookkeeping. Others will be credited in the next book. It is impossible to credit all the people who have served on the board and contributed so faithfully.

My mission colleagues and Thai church leaders, who guided me in adapting to a new culture, and shared in helping me evaluate and understand these experiences in ministry.

Gloria Drahn for her encouragement, typing and editing in the initial stages, which enabled me to put some thoughts on paper. Sylvia Gorsuch for reading through the early manuscript, contributing ideas and the assurance that it was worthwhile.

Somkit Buarawong for her responsible, diligent research.

Karen Thomson, Rob Collins, Susan Offner, Doris Redd, Adele Anderson and Doris Jane Pappenhagen for their valuable comments and suggestions.

Anita Schulenburg for typing and revising.This book would not have been published without her commitment and constructive feedback.

CONTENTS

INTRODUCTION

"That which was from the beginning, which we have heard, which we have seen with our eyes, which we have looked at and our own hands have touched—this we proclaim concerning the Word of life...so that you also may have fellowship with us. And our fellowship is with the Father and his Son, Jesus Christ. We write this to make our joy complete." 1 Jn. 1:1, 3, 4

Many people have doubts that there really is a God above all gods, a Holy Spirit who loves and cares for all of us personally through Jesus Christ. I have written this book to share my experiences and those of many others who cried out to God in times of crises and knew that they had been answered.

In the doubts, perplexities, and troubles of life, these people turned to God and found reassurance, light, and comfort. Jesus does honor his word in Matthew 7:7, "Ask and it will be given to you; seek and you will find; knock and the door will be opened to you." Jesus is not only urging believers to have confidence in prayer, but this promise is for non-believers as well.

People accept Christ for various reasons, depending on the needs at a particular time in their lives. These true stories gleaned from 42 years of mission in Thailand, illustrate how God answers prayer for those who are sincere in their requests. People have experienced the reality and presence of God through answered prayer. That experience has transformed their lives and has also led to change in others.

There is an old hymn true to life's experience: "It is no secret what God can do. What He's done for others, He'll do for you." We believe God will speak with you when you sincerely ask, seek, and knock, just as He has with us. We have seen the power of God in the gospel to redeem, deliver, fulfill, and make whole. We are compelled to share this gospel and these life experiences "to make our joy complete."

Many Christians are not sure how to begin sharing the good news. I hope that after reading this book Christians will be encouraged to invite their friends who do not know God to test the promise in Mt. 7:7, by asking God to help them in their times of need.

The Biblical account in Acts records how people heard the gospel, but also how they experienced signs and wonders. People must hear the message. Many, if not most, also need a personal experience before they can make a full commitment. This is especially true in areas where belief in the one true God, known through Jesus Christ, requires a break with predominant worldview.

Chapter 1 begins with accounts of people confirming the reality of God through prayer, causing them to commit their lives to Christ. Even though some of their requests were often very strange, each one experienced God's presence in the answer. That answer became an anchor in their lives. God meets us where we are.

Chapter 2 is about purpose and meaning. This is my own testimony of how God answered my question, "Lord, Why Am I Here?" I offer my witness as an encouragement for others to ask and receive the answers as to why they are here.

Chapters 3, 4, and 5 give examples of people asking and receiving what is generally understood as salvation, i.e. deliverance from sin, Satan and death.

Chapter 6 concerns God's help to live triumphantly through trouble and suffering. In many interviews with new Christians in Thailand, the persons indicated that they had heard the gospel, or had seen good Christian examples. However, it was only after an answer to prayer in time of trouble that each one could make a definite decision to accept Jesus as Lord and Savior.

Chapter 7 discusses healing prayer. **Chapter 8** gives examples of how God has worked in history to answer the cries of the oppressed for freedom and justice. **Chapter 9** is a plea for holiness.

The Gospel must be expressed in ways that are easily understood. I have been intimately involved with the lives of the people in this book, and have shared their stories in a personal and direct way. Where a person's name is used, permission was granted. In some stories I have used only their first names to avoid close identification and possible embarrassment to their relatives. Scriptures are selected to illustrate these stories.

I believe that God is Spirit and not bound by any sexual gender. I have decided to use the male personal pronoun in reference to God because it is Biblical and historical in the English language. It helps avoid repetitive and awkward sentence structure.

CHAPTER 1

GOD! IF YOU ARE REALLY GOD...

CONFIRMING GOD'S REALITY - Background

"Gideon replied, 'If now I have found favor in your eyes, give me a sign that it is really you talking to me.'" Jdg. 6:17

We want people to know and experience the saving love of God through Jesus Christ. However, where we live, people often feel that we merely want them to exchange a foreign teaching for their own. They think that to believe in God would require a radical break with their own culture. We have found that one of the best ways to interest others in believing in God is to tell them that God loves them and will help them in their troubles. If they do pray, and they feel that God answers that prayer, then they begin to believe. When they have experienced God, then it is not so hard for them to accept that the best way to know God is through Jesus.

It takes something dramatic to cause them to change—either signs or wonders or some crisis in their lives. Often, even if they have seen signs and wonders, they are like Gideon and still need answers to personal prayers before they will make a commitment. There are exceptions, but I believe that most of those who make a full commitment to Christ do so because God answered their prayers, or they may make a tentative commitment in the expectation that God will answer their prayers.

When we present the traditional gospel message of Jesus Christ's death and resurrection, we should also present the challenge that they test out what we say by asking God to help them in time of need.

In my experience, most people did not become believers primarily to receive forgiveness of sin. The major exceptions were bandits or thugs who knew they were gross sinners. Ordinary people think that they are not so bad and that they can make up for whatever wrong they have done by doing good. In Thailand, this is known as making merit.

We may fear that people may ask for something that is unreasonable or not good. However, Jesus' example in Luke 11:5-8 about asking the friend for bread at midnight, followed by the promise "ask and it will be given to you" vs. 9-13, is given without any qualification whatsoever. If God's word makes this promise, how dare we qualify it? Even though I say this, I still find it hard to resist qualifying the statement with, "I don't think God wants you to ask for a lottery number."

Ever since childhood I have been taught not to tempt or test God by asking for too much. The scriptural authority for this is Jesus' quote of Dt. 6:16 in resisting the temptation of the devil. (Mt. 4:7 and Lk. 4: 12) "Do not put the Lord your God to the test." Certainly, there is truth in this, but I now believe the main meaning is that Jesus was resisting being compelled to use his power.

Jesus did refer to his works and miracles as evidence of being the Messiah. When John the Baptist asked if he was the one who was to come, Jesus replied, "The blind receive sight, the lame walk, those who have leprosy are cured, the deaf hear, the dead are raised, . . ." (Mt. 11:5). Fourteen passages in John's Gospel refer to signs that attested to Jesus power and lead to belief (Jn.2:23; 3:2; 4:54; 6:2,14,26,30; 7:31; 9:16; 10:41; 11:47; 12:18,37; 20:30)

The culminating sign is the resurrection. Acts has many references to signs and wonders that accompany preaching. Of course many did not believe even though they saw signs. It is our privilege to ask but the answer is up to God.

It is true that a person may not believe because they didn't get what they asked for. It is the same when we preach or give personal witnesses to people, and they don't respond. Our work is to do the best we can to offer the best we have, which is the saving love of God through Jesus Christ. We must trust God for their response.

On my first furlough in1965- 66, I had a stimulating year at Yale University, evaluating our experiences and discussing theological problems from many different points of view. One of the theological fads at that time was "God is Dead Theology," which pronounced that God is no longer in heaven, but incarnate in human beings. Therefore, there is no need to pray to God as though God is "out there somewhere."

When I returned to the field, I discussed this with Dr. Kenneth Wells, Ph.D., a long-time missionary who, at that time, was head of the Christian Literature Department of the Church of Christ in Thailand. He said to me, "The reason I know God is not dead is that he answers my prayers."

As a young impressionable seminary student, I remember one professor saying, "We don't need to bother God with little things. He has much more important work to do." My experience is different. God is love, and real love is interested in little things. When my grandchild asks for something, no matter how small, I seriously consider how to respond.

For a while the movement against any supernatural expression went so far in the U.S. that one seminary offered a summer course entitled "The Possibility of Prayer in a Secular Age." The view that God is not concerned with little things is often advanced by those who have asked for something very important, and they did not get what they wanted. Also, there are people who deny God, because they feel their prayers were not answered.

Many times God does say, "No." or "Wait." by his silence. But a majority of those that I know in Thailand, made a decision to follow Christ because of answered prayer. Jesus urges us to ask, and we should not hesitate to do so. "You do not have, because you do not ask God." (Jas. 4:2). We must trust God to answer in the appropriate way for that person at that time.

Bud and Patsy Porter (front) came to visit us and went along with Joan, David (center), and other Christians to share the reality of God with the Lao Song people during flood season. Allan took the picture. (1966)

GOD, IF YOU'RE REALLY GOD...

Joan at 3

**"Where can I go from your Spirit?
Where can I flee from your presence?"
Ps. 139:7**

Whenever my wife, Joan, is called upon to give her testimony she begins with her experience in Houston, Texas, when she was twelve years old. At that time her father had become an alcoholic, and was dangerous to the three children when he came home drunk. When he was sober he was a loving supportive father, but his behavior changed radically when under the influence of alcohol.

One evening, Joan's mother told her that she would have to get a divorce, and Joan's world was shattered. She stumbled out into the World War II victory garden in the back yard. It was just at dusk, and the huge Texas sky was filling with stars. Joan said:

In show biz at 8

"I felt so small and the universe was so big. I thought, 'Why was I born? What's the meaning of my life?' I cried out in the dark, 'God, if you're really God, let me know it.' I didn't see anything or hear anything, but it was as if someone put loving arms around me. I felt relief and peace."

Joan went back into the house and somehow turned to Psalms 139:7, "Where can I go from your Spirit? Where can I flee from your presence?" She knew she was not alone and never would be. This experience has become a benchmark in her life. Joan's mother and father divorced. The family went through many struggles, but the assurance of that night never deserted her. It stayed with her as she rose to success on Broadway, national television, and leading roles in London and Belgium.

After 42 years of missionary work in Thailand, this first confirming presence of God has never left her. One of the favorite songs from her Broadway musical days still is "You'll Never Walk Alone." The story of how I came into Joan's life and found meaning for my own life is found in chapter 2, "Love at First Sight."

Allan, 8, biding his time

Joan in London at 24

HELP ME FIND MY FRIEND

"Ask and it will be given to you; seek and you will find; knock and the door will be opened to you." Mt. 7:7

"Praise be to God, who has not rejected my prayer nor withheld his love from me!" Ps. 66:20

The first time I realized the importance of Jesus' promise to ask and receive, knock and it will be opened, seek and you will find, was when I read Achan Samrit Wongsan's book in Thai about Achan Puang Akkapin (Achan means "respected teacher.") The English translation of the title is *The Respected Teacher with No Degree: Achan Puang Akkapin.* (Bk. 1, Urban-Industrial Life Div., The Church of Christ in Thailand, Bangkok 1970).

Achan Samrit tells how Achan Puang became a Christian. He was born in Nakhon Phanom Province in 1893. As a young boy he drifted around and got in with a bad crowd in Laos. Later he went to Bangkok, lived in a temple, and worked as a clerk. It was a job he didn't like, and he wasn't able to make any money. He knew a friend had come to Bangkok, and he thought that friend could help him find a better opportunity. As he wandered around the streets of the big city, he looked in a shop and saw a western lady teaching. He stopped to listen. Mrs. McCord, a missionary, was teaching about God from the book of Jonah.

He didn't think too much about what she had said, but later he passed by the shop again. This time on the board above the missionary's head in big letters were the words "ASK AND RECEIVE." He walked inside and listened carefully as she taught from the Bible. Then he asked her, "If God is real, pray for me to find my friend." She led him in a prayer, and he began searching again. Three days later, as he walked in the market, suddenly someone bumped into him. He backed away, irritated.

Then he saw it was the friend he was searching for, and he cried out, "Thank God." He took his friend back to that storefront. Now he was a believer and wanted to learn more about this God who had answered his prayer.

Achan Puang went on to become a powerful evangelist. He initiated the model for the yearly weeks of evangelism in the Christian schools, which is still followed. Many of the Christian leaders in the united church, The Church of Christ in Thailand (CCT), made decisions for Christ during those weeks.

After World War II, Achan Puang was elected Moderator of the CCT, leading the church to more independence from mission organizations. His son, Achan Pisanu, was the head of the Christian Education Department of the CCT for many years and is a prominent Christian writer. On May 19, 1963, Achan Puang fell dead in the pulpit from a heart attack at the age of 70. He was preaching in the Supan Luang (Yellow Bridge) Chinese Church in Bangkok.

Achan Puang's conversion through God's answer to his prayer opened up a new approach for me—challenging people to ask and receive.

Achan Puang Akkapin

SICK AND ALONE   (David)

**"Hear my prayer, O Lord; let my cry for help come to you....
I lie awake; I have become like a bird alone on a housetop."
Ps. 102:1, 7**

People often say to us "you have made a lot of sacrifices to go overseas as missionaries." We do not feel that we have sacrificed at all. Sometimes we are embarrassed because our life has been so much easier than we expected. However, there is one time when I really feel we made a sacrifice. That was when we made the hard decision to send our eight-year old son 500 miles north to live in the mission hostel. He would begin the second grade in the small international school in Chiang Mai, where there were trusted and dedicated house parents.

Joan homeschooling David in the first grade

Joan had taught him at our home in the little village of Sam Yaek located about fifty miles west of Bangkok. (For fifty years the mission has spelled the locality, Sam Yek, but that does not give the true sound, so I have changed to the Thai government usage of Sam Yaek)

In teaching David, Joan used a standard correspondence course, but it took one and one-half years to get him through the first grade. There were so many people around all the time that Joan just couldn't concentrate on teaching.

We had never considered having to send our children away for school. In the little town where I grew up, I felt that if someone sent their child away for schooling it must be because the family had broken up, the child was too hard to handle, or possibly the parents didn't want him or her.

Now I realize that is not a fair assessment, but I never thought I would send my own children away. Again and again I would come home to find both mother and son in tears of frustration. After much agonizing and praying, I persuaded Joan that we needed to send David to Chiang Mai.

I'll never forget the sad four-hour drive to Bangkok and the awful wrench when we put David on the plane. Two months later, I received expense money to fly up to Chiang Mai for a meeting and was able to bring David to stay with me in a missionary's home. David slept beside me in a double bed. The morning I was to fly back, David woke me sobbing on my chest. You can imagine how I felt. It still hurts when I think of it. One of the hardest things I have ever had to do was to take him back to school, say goodbye, and get on the plane.

David was able to come home for three days during the American Thanksgiving holidays. Sunday morning church services were held in the school pavilion. We had begun giving invitations every week, and people were walking to the front to make confessions of faith.

That morning we were singing the usual dedication hymn "Just as I Am" translated into Thai. No one came forward, so on the last verse I asked the congregation to close their eyes, pray and rededicate themselves as they hummed. While we hummed and prayed, I heard footsteps. I wanted to peek, but I was praying so I didn't. When the verse was over, I opened my eyes and there was David. I was very surprised and asked him why he had come. He replied, "When I went to Chiang Mai, I was so homesick I cried. I felt sick and alone. Then I cried out, 'Jesus, if you're real, take away my homesickness,' and He did. So I want to give my life to Jesus."

David ,8, baptism at Sam Yaek Church (1970)

Now, 34 years later, he is still giving his life to Jesus as a missionary. (See chap. 4, "Who Are You Serving Now?")

Captain David Eubank jumps with his HALO unit carrying a
Thai flag as part of a joint exercise with the Thai Special Forces
in Udon, Thailand, 1992

A SCIENTIFIC EXPERIMENT

"If you then, though you are evil, know how to give good gifts to your children, how much more will your Father in heaven give the Holy Spirit to those who ask him!" Luke 11:13

In February 1994, we had to begin the return journey by bus across southwestern China, after visiting the Wa tribe along the China-Burma border. Our party understood we were to wake up at 5:00 a.m. We were greatly distressed when our Chinese police officer friend knocked on the door and woke us up saying, "The bus was supposed to leave at 5:00 a.m. and I am holding it for you." Frantically we dressed, packed and rushed to the bus station as fast as we could. The bus had been waiting almost an hour before we finally got there, and we were very embarrassed.

When we climbed in the bus, there was a lot of commotion. I bowed deeply with a Thai "wai," putting my hands together before my face as in prayer while bowing several times. I also threw up my hands and pleaded, "We are sorry, we are sorry, we are sorry." The people saw my animated actions and began to laugh. I felt somewhat relieved and sat down.

Surprisingly, the young Chinese man beside me began to speak in excellent English. I asked him, "What can I do for these people for being so late?" He gave me a reassuring smile and said, "It's all right, they have forgiven you." He offered a hard-boiled egg, which I took, and gave him an apple in return. I had a strong feeling of love for the Chinese people at that moment.

When I asked the student about himself, he told me he was about to graduate from the Technological College in Kunming, with a degree in physics. He said he hoped to take a test and qualify for a scholarship. The scholarship would enable him to study for a master's degree at a prestigious technical institute in Beijing. He was obviously intelligent and very articulate. I told him that I believed he should be able to get the scholarship.

Then he asked me, "What do you do?" I braced myself and replied, "Well really, I want people to know about God." He responded from his strong Communist training, "We Chinese don't need religion. We have science." After praying inwardly how to speak to him, I told him that I had been a geological engineer with some background in science. Then I tried to use some of the old classic arguments for belief in God, i.e. first cause, purpose, etc. I gave him the old example of a person seeing a clock for the first time and asking, "Could this clock come about accidentally?"

I told him when I was a child my grandmother gave me a broken alarm clock. I was proud of myself because I could take it completely apart, but then getting it back together was a different matter. Finally, frustrated, I put everything in a box and started shaking it. Then I asked the student, "How many times do you think I would have to shake that box for all the parts to come back into order, wind themselves up and begin ticking." It is really a lot easier to think that a mind created that clock than to think it could come together accidentally. He just laughed and did not show much response.

Then I shared my own short testimony of how I heard the still small voice which confirmed that God is, and that I had to be a missionary (See chap 2, "Where Are Your Doubts Now?") He listened politely, but I saw no reaction.

We talked about other things, and every once in a while I inwardly asked God what to say. Then I thought of a different approach. I said, "You are a scientist and believe in the scientific method. A scientist has to put away any prejudice, and be willing to test solutions to a problem and accept what works. I propose a scientific experiment for you. It doesn't cost anything and requires very little time. Try asking, 'God, are you really here? I really want to know.' God has spoken to people in different ways throughout history. Their experiences are recorded in the Bible. I just shared how God spoke to me. Now, if you ask, God will speak to you in a way that's appropriate for you."

The young man did not say anything, but somehow his demeanor made me feel he was interested. We carried on a friendly conversation until we got off the bus. We agreed that we would meet again for breakfast in our hotel in Kunming, before I flew back to Chiang Mai. His college was just across the lake from where I was staying. After breakfast, I gave him my address and reminded him again, "Don't forget to try that experiment." He just smiled and made a slight nod.

In April I received a letter from him in Chiang Mai. It said,

> I waited to write to you until after I learned about my tests for the master's scholarship. Now I know: I failed. I needed 500 points to pass in physics. I made that, but I had to have 50 points in political science. I don't know anything about political science, and I only made 48. I missed the scholarship by two points. But don't worry about me. God will take care of my character.

He wrote a little more to say that he had a job with a computer manufacturer, and he closed by saying, "May God bless you." I replied to his letter and heard from him once more affirming his faith. Then I lost touch.

That experience has given me the confidence to offer this experiment to others. If a person sincerely asks, God will answer.

The Wa tribal chief gives our group a warm welcome to their village in eastern Burma - David, Karen, Allan and others were returning from visiting this area when Allan met the Chinese student told about in this story.

KEEP THE BIRDS OUT OF MY FIELD

"For everyone who asks receives; he who seeks finds; and to him who knocks the door will be opened. Which of you, when his son asks for bread, will give him a stone? Or if he asks for a fish, will give him a snake?" Mt. 7:8-10

One Sunday in 1966, during the early days of our work at Sam Yaek, Nakhon Pathom Province, Nai Hawm surprised us by showing up for the church service. He had ridden his bicycle over 15 miles to get there. We had met him through Lamut, the bandit, and Mother Tiger, (See chap. 3). He was a member of Mother Tiger's gang. She had come to give her life to Christ a few weeks earlier. Like her, Nai Hawm found a seat on the back row. We sang "Just as I Am" as an invitation hymn, and Nai Hawm came walking up to the front. He said:

> You told me that God answers prayer, and it is true. It is nearly time for rice harvest. Early this week, I was out since dawn chasing the birds out of my fields. The birds would fly up and land in my neighbor's field.

> My neighbor has more money than I do, and he has an explosive device that goes, 'boom.' The birds would fly right back to light in my field. I chased them out over and over all morning. Finally, I was exhausted. I had not eaten. I have ulcers, and my stomach was killing me.

> Then, I remembered what you had said about God answering prayer. I spoke out loud and said, 'God if you are really here, look after my field, and don't let the birds get the crop while I get some breakfast.'

> I went home to eat. After breakfast I came outside, and there was not one bird in my field. They were all over in my neighbor's field. The 'boom' would sound, and the

birds would fly up, circle over my field and light right back down in his field. God does answer prayer, and I want to give my life to Jesus.

I would not have dared to suggest that he pray like that, but he was convinced of God's care for him. He had two girls and later, after baptism, he asked us to pray with him for a boy. We did, and we were all excited when a boy was born.

Nai Hawm and his wife, Nang Paen,
at their baptism in Sam Yaek. (1967)
Allan and Achan Bamrung Adipat (back)

A year later, the boy came down with pneumonia and died. We did not hear about the illness in time to get him to the hospital. Even then, Nai Hawm remained strong in his faith and led others to believe. God had dramatically answered his first prayer. That experience remained with him, even after his later prayer ended so tragically.

We moved north to Chiang Mai to teach in what is now known as McGilvary Faculty of Theology, Payap University. I heard that Nai Hawm and his wife had worked as janitors and gardeners at the Thai church in Nakhon Pathom city. They had a bad experience with a pastor who was later dismissed on moral grounds. They moved back to their home area, and no one knew what happened to them.

More than 10 years passed by, and we went to help his old friend, Lamut, open a new chapel. Lamut said Nai Hawm and his wife still believed. I had a lot of doubts because of their bad experience in the church and lack of contact with other Christians through these years.

Achan Bamrung, the first elder of Sam Yaek church, and I went out to find them. We found leads on three Nai Hawms in that area. The first two were not the Nai Hawm we were seeking. We followed directions to the third house and stopped to confirm that the next house was Nai Hawm's home. We asked, "Is there a Nai Hawm living next door?" The neighbor immediately replied, "Oh, you mean the Nai Hawm who is Christian?" It was so good to restore fellowship with Nai Hawm and his wife once more.

We have known many others like Nai Hawm, who have remained followers of Christ, even when at a later time they did not receive what they asked for.

Wasunchai (Sunshine) and Yurium
after their marriage.

Yurium as the older daughter (right), Somkit as the younger
sister (left), and Sawitree as the mother, in "The Prodigal
Daughter" Likay

MAKE ME FALL IN LOVE

**"...God has surely listened and heard my voice in prayer."
Ps. 66:19**

Thai Folk Drama (Likay) began as an experiment to communicate the gospel of Jesus Christ in ways easily understood in Thai culture. We started with seminary students in Payap University, Thailand's first Christian university. An extra dancer was needed to be one of the angels, carrying Lazarus up to heaven to be beside Abraham (Lk. 16:19-22). Kajon (See chap. 6, "That Piece of Glass") knew a good dancer in the university who wasn't a Christian, but had good character. She came and began to travel with us on weekends at every opportunity.

By the time Yurium graduated the next year, we had a budget for some full-time performers to begin the Christian Communications Institute (CCI) as a department in Payap University. Even though she had not become Christian, she was so compatible and able that we hired her. We trusted that God was going to call her.

Every once in a while, I tried to help God by asking Yurium if she was ready yet to make a decision. Even though I was her employer, she finally was fed up with my pushing and said very strongly, "Don't ask me anymore about this. When I decide, I'll let you know." I bit my lip, prayed and waited.

Yurium in Classical Thai
Dance Costume

Three years passed. One day she told me "I have decided. I believe and am ready to become Christian." I asked her what happened. Even at this writing, I find it very difficult to believe her answer. Here is her reply:

I had two tests to see if God was real. First, I challenged, 'God, if you are real, make me fail a course.' I have never failed one in my life, and sure enough – during my senior year I failed a course. The second test was about Sunshine (nickname). He had been trying to court me and I did not like him at all. I wished he would leave me alone. Finally, I was so frustrated that I cried out, 'God if you are really God, make me fall in love with that man that I don't like at all,' It happened. I fell deeply in love.

Not long afterwards, she was baptized and engaged to Wasunchai (Sunshine) Im-ote. They asked me to perform their wedding ceremony. She has been through many ups and downs, but that love has lasted for more than 20 years. Now she is the Assistant Director of the CCI, and Sunshine teaches music in Payap University.

Recently, when I went to Yurium for permission to write her testimony, I asked her again, "Were those answers to prayers about failing a course and falling in love with Sunshine the real reasons you decided to become Christian?" She smiled and said, "Yes!"

Previously, I would not have dared to tell people to pray as they did in the foregoing stories. Now, I have come to believe that Matthew 7:7 and Luke 11:9 "Ask and it will be given you…" are two of the most powerful evangelistic verses in the Bible. Jesus made the promise, and we can trust him to honor his word.

CHAPTER 2

WHY AM I HERE? – Purpose & Meaning

"Before I formed you in the womb I knew you, before you were born I set you apart..." Jer.1:5

"For we are God's workmanship, created in Christ Jesus to do good works, which God prepared in advance for us to do Eph. 2:10

LOVE AT FIRST SIGHT

"...you have stolen my heart with one glance of your eyes..." Song of Solomon 4:9

"Above all, love each other deeply, because love covers over a multitude of sins." 1 Pet. 4:8

By March of 1953, I had been in Korea a year and was commanding "A" Company, 11th Engineer Combat Battalion. My unit was blasting a road through the mountains to build a secondary defensive position. It was a lonely and isolated location. The battalion commander, probably feeling sorry for us, sent a small USO troupe to entertain us. We enthusiastically built a stage in our mess hall.

The troupe arrived. As they walked into the mess hall, I was struck by one particularly pretty face. She added something special to the GI uniform she was wearing. After changing into something more fitting, She sang "Oklahoma," and I could feel myself sinking. After the show, we had a chance to get acquainted and discovered that we were both from Texas. Joan Hovis was from Houston. I was from Dallas.

When it came time to send them back to group headquarters where they were staying, I wanted to take Joan back myself, but I remembered my prior decision. I came to Korea knowing that most soldiers were rotated home after about a year. I decided, "If I don't write any letters to girls or put up pin-up pictures, I will be all right for a year."

Joan's USO Troupe performing for the Engineers

My plan was successful until I went to a Bob Hope Show and saw all those lovely girls. I came back feeling depressed, because I realized what I was missing. Concerning Joan, I thought, "Allan, this is a hopeless situation. Why prolong the agony?" I had another lieutenant take her back.

The next day was Wednesday. After lunch the chaplain came for our regular time of worship before the men went back to work. In order to set a good example, I always tried to attend.

But usually I was so tired that as soon as I sat down and relaxed, I invariably went to sleep. This was very embarrassing, but the chaplain was kind and never mentioned it.

That day at lunch, before worship, the chaplain told me, "Joan said to tell you that if you are anywhere around--come see her." Even today, Joan still cannot believe she said that. But would a chaplain lie? In any case, that invitation was all it took. The chaplain told me that the troupe was performing at M.A.S.H.(Mobile Army Surgical Hospital) that afternoon. I think I skipped worship and jumped into my jeep.

The hospital closely resembled the sets of a popular television show about life in Korea called, "M.A.S.H." Just as in the TV show, the doctors here were pretty wild. They were excellent doctors, but because they were under such pressure during battles, they often blew off steam when it was quiet. The battlefront had stabilized, and my unit was in charge of pouring cement floors to get the operating rooms and wards up out of the mud. Since the USO was going to be there, I felt it my "duty" to check out the structures.

As I parked my jeep, I told myself, "Allan, you're just wasting your time." I walked up to the tent where the show was going on. Joan was standing outside talking to two officers. I walked up to them. She remembered me. After a few weak words, I offered, "Is there anything I can do for you?"

Surprisingly, she said, "Yes! You can drive me to the Turk unit for our next show." My heart leaped. Her escort officer quickly squelched that hope with, "You can't do that. It's against the rules." I lamely tried once more, "Well, is there any thing else?" Amazingly, she said, "Yes! Tomorrow is my day off. I haven't had time to go through the wards to visit the wounded yet. Could you take me?" Being commander made it easy for me to get off, so the next day I picked up Joan at the Division

Headquarters and began our drive to the hospital. Then Joan said, "I have a jeep driver's license. May I drive?" At that point, I would have allowed almost anything. I moved over and let her take the wheel. She started down the compacted dirt main supply route to the front.

About halfway there, she looked over and said, "You aren't nervous at all are you?" "No," I honestly replied. But I no sooner got the "No." out of my mouth, than Joan drove too close to the wet muddy shoulders. The jeep slid on its side into the ditch. As I crawled out, who should stop to help, but a truckload of my men patrolling and maintaining that portion of the road. They walked over with smirks on their faces. They all remembered Joan, of course. Effortlessly, they surrounded the vehicle and lifted it back up on the road. I took over the driving, and we had a good visit with the wounded.

Joan & Allan at M.A.S.H. (March, 1953)

I had a relay phone connection to my company, so I called and asked the mess Sergeant to fix a little dinner for Joan and me. On the 30-minute drive to my headquarters, I realized, that besides being beautiful and having an enchanting singing voice, Joan truly had fine character.

It suddenly came to my mind, "I want to marry this girl." Then I thought, "How dumb! There must be a thousand lonely GIs attracted to this wholesome, lovely young woman." I was in a kind of daze throughout the cozy candlelight dinner for two, which my mess sergeant and my executive officer had arranged. After dinner I drove Joan back to her quarters, stole one kiss and sadly said goodbye. Again, I had that sinking feeling. That experience was expressed very well in the words of a song Joan liked to sing, "You're not sick. You're just in love."

Joan promised to write, and she did. The month after her intrusion into my life, I was sent for a five day R & R (rest and recuperation) leave to Japan. I went to the Post Exchange in Tokyo and almost bought her an engagement ring, but I knew that was too stupid. However, I did buy a string of expensive Mikimoto pearls for her. She did not see them or know about them for six years.

Joan, after she changed into something more fitting
and sang "Oklahoma" for Allan's unit

Joan received the Theatre World Award as one of the ten most "Promising Personalities" of the 1957-58 Broadway season. (Please forgive my boasting, but the Lord has given me no greater gift than Joan – see 2 Cor. 11:16-21)

MAKING A MILLION

**"For where your treasure is, there your heart will be also."
Mt. 6:21**

In August, 1953, eight days after the Korean cease-fire, I was standing on the bank of the same river where I had spent my first night a year and a half earlier (see chap 5, "It's All Right"). The front had been stabilized. Because of flooding, three bridges had been washed out. We could not build high bridges because they would come under enemy fire.

I was supervising construction of a fourth bridge when I received word that I could go back to the States. I jumped in my jeep and packed my duffel bag. Other capable hands could continue the construction. I boarded a troop ship, sailed back through the Golden Gate Bridge in San Francisco and flew home.

The Army assigned me to River and Harbor Control with the Corps of Engineers' office in New Orleans. My job would be inspection of flood control construction on the Intercoastal Waterway and the Mississippi River.

Before reporting for work, I called Joan's home and learned that she was singing in the musical "Brigadoon" in Houston. I arranged to spend three days there on the pretext of exploring job possibilities with a major oil company that had offered a job before I entered the service. When I contacted them they assured me they would still hire me.

With the job inquiries out of the way, I got down to business with Joan. When I saw her sparkling eyes on stage singing "Waiting For My Dearie" I thought, "She is waiting for me, but she doesn't know it."

Picnicking with Joan, brother Tommy, sister Janet and the
new Chevy. in Spring Branch, Houston. (August 1953)

As we parted, that old sinking feeling came back because
I did not see how our future could work out. I went on to New
Orleans, and Joan left for Hollywood with an engagement at the
Coconut Grove. While there, she performed in several national
TV shows including, "The Ford Theater," and "The Lone
Ranger".

That year in Louisiana was significant for me. I observed
the extreme contrast between the sophisticated and lively New
Orleans atmosphere and the Cajun country swamp and shrimp
boat culture of Morgan City, where I spent most of my time. I
was inspecting a boat lock for the Inter-coastal Waterway
System.

It was a pleasure working with capable, dedicated, and
honest civilian engineers who wanted to get the most for the
Government's money. If we ate with a contractor, we paid for
our own meal. That way we would not feel obligated to them in
any respect. If we received nothing from them personally, we
were free to hold them to the exact details of construction,

ensuring a lasting job. These men were not ashamed to admit that their morality came from their Christian faith. It made me see the impact of Christian morality in everyday life. Knowing that God is personal and is watching us all the time certainly helped keep me honest.

While in New Orleans, I became an active member of the St. Charles Ave. Christian Church. One day while alone in my apartment, a voice "out of the blue," said, "You are to be a missionary!"

It came with the penetrating power of God and burned into my mind. I did not argue. I cannot remember thinking of being a minister or missionary before, but now it seemed exactly right. I was ready to do it, but not yet. I tried to bargain: "All right, Lord, I am willing, but I can do a lot more for you rich than I can poor. Let me make a million dollars in the oil business first, and then I can go all out for you."

I didn't hear any response, but I thought we had made a deal. My three-year commitment as a regular army officer was up in June 1954. I enjoyed the army life and could have made it a career, but now I had a new purpose. I was ready to move on. Since I planned to make my million first, I did not tell anyone of my call but submitted my resignation.

After my discharge in August, I drove to Houston and had several interviews with oil companies. I decided to work for Standard Oil Company of Texas because I could work in my hometown of Dallas, and they offered me 25 dollars more per month.

With that settled, I took a plane to Los Angeles to see Joan. Since my visit to Houston, we had been corresponding. I would write one month, and she would answer the next. Then, I would wait another month to answer. She had given me one of

43

her pin-up pictures, which I always kept on my desk. In the spring, Joan wrote inviting me to come out for a visit. I wrote back, "The only reason I will come that far is to see if we are going to get married."

Joan in Hollywood (1954)

Joan replied, "That is not what I meant, but if you want to come out just for a visit you are welcome."

The visit was less than rewarding. Joan was appearing on the Ray Milland Show that week, and she had to call her agent about other jobs every hour. I quickly saw that life as a "stage door Johnny" was not for me. Joan was interested in a career on Broadway, and the oil business held no attractions for her. I did not tell her about my call to be a missionary. She didn't think I was very spiritual, because I got bored listening to her read Kahil Gibran's *The Prophet.* It seemed too syrupy at the time.

After a week, I had had enough. There was no future in this. I decided, "This is not the girl for me, but there has to be someone like her out there somewhere." I determined to get out of Los Angeles that day. I called the airport and found there was a strike, and no planes were flying. I bought a train ticket, but found the train had a day layover in El Paso. I answered a share-the-ride ad, but the driver could never get enough riders. I finally got on a bus that night. We had a flat tire in the desert on the edge of Lordsburg, New Mexico. I got out, walked into town, and bought some copper ore earrings to give my sister on her birthday. When I got out of the store, I found the bus had left.

My bag with my traveler's checks was in the bus. I tried to hitchhike, but no one would pick me up. With the little cash I had, I called El Paso and told them to take my bags off the bus. Then, I bought a ticket on a different bus line to El Paso. In El Paso, I got my bag with the traveler's checks and bought a ticket the rest of the way to Dallas. It had taken two full frustrating days to get home.

I thought that terrible trip was the cap on a bad decision to go out to Hollywood stargazing. The showgirl escapade was over. Now, I could settle down and make my million.

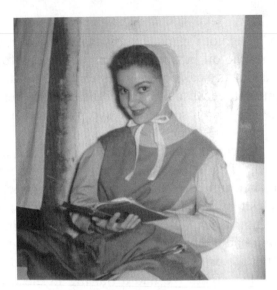

Joan reading her Bible backstage.
"Plain and Fancy"
Theater Royale, Drury Lane, London (1956)

Joan in "Wonderful Town" at the World's Fair, Brussels, Belgium
(1958)

WHERE ARE YOUR DOUBTS NOW?

"But seek first the kingdom and his righteousness, and all these things will be given to you as well." Mt. 6:33

At least 50 of my A & M classmates were out of the service, single and living in Dallas. Together we enjoyed three fun years on the debutante stag trail. As a geologist, I was learning the oil business, dreaming of a prosperous future, and looking for oil in the East Texas district. I even found some oil for my company.

Once I was very disappointed when the company said one of my prospects was too small for them to make a profit. In order to work with an oil company, geologists must sign a paper promising that they will not go into private oil business on the side, and that all prospects they find belong to the company. This time, I was tempted to sell it to an independent oilman (a friend from college days.) I told myself, "The company doesn't want it anyway, so it won't hurt them. A lot of geologists have gotten rich by ignoring that promise, and besides, who would know until I had already struck it rich?"

Then came the little voice, "What would your father do?" Dad was my role model for integrity. I also thought, "God is with me and watching." Even though my goal was a million dollars, I called the friend and told him, "I can't go through with the deal." I never did found out if there really was oil on that prospect.

During this time I was actively attending the 4000-member East Dallas Christian Church with my parents. Joan passed through Dallas a couple of times and called. We went out one night. She even called my parents when I was out of town and stayed that night at my home. She still doesn't know why she did that. I still thought it was over between us. The last time I heard from her, she was on her way to London. She had a lead role in an American musical, "Plain and Fancy," at the Theatre Royal, Drury Lane there.

The work was good and so was the company, but I still had my million dollar dream. After three years, I asked for a transfer to the West Texas Production Department, so I could get some drilling experience. Oil was booming. The best way to make lots of money was to own your own wells.

Oil Drilling Rig

I needed drilling experience to do this, so I asked to be transferred to west Texas. I was sent to the Yates Field in Iraan, Texas. It was one of the most prolific oil fields in Texas. When they first found oil in 1927, the land was only good for sheep. Ira and Ann Yates had owned it originally. When the gushers came in they named the town, "Iraan," after them. There were about 700 people in the town, and I lived three miles outside in an oil camp. I liked the country, the work, and the people, but a single man does get lonesome.

I thought again about Joan and sent her a Christmas card. About the same time, I read the scripture, Matthew 6:33, "Seek first his kingdom..." I slammed the Bible shut. "How can I get a million dollars in front of the kingdom?" I asked myself. That scripture was no longer only in the book. Now it was in my heart, and I could not get rid of it. That is why the Bible is called the "Word of God."

In June of 1957, while I was in Dallas, James Earl Owen came to East Dallas Christian Church promoting missions and recruiting candidates. He was the first person I told about my interest in missions. He gave me a thick stack of application forms. At the time, I felt there were too many forms to fill out, so I filed them. Now it was January of 1958. With new conviction, I dug out the file and laboriously filled out the forms. Then, I sent them off to the Division of Overseas Ministries of the Christian Church (Disciples of Christ) in Indianapolis, Indiana, saying only that I was exploring mission possibilities. Ralph Palmer was now in charge of recruiting and training missionaries. He invited me to drive 400 miles northeast to Dallas to meet him. I drove up on Saturday. Before I opened Ralph's screen door, I told him, "I am not sure if I want to be a missionary." He immediately retorted, "That's all right. We are not sure we want you either."

Another appointment was made to fly up to Oklahoma to be interviewed by a psychiatrist and take a battery of psychological tests. The psychologist recommended a book, *Human Destiny* by Lacomte du Nouy, who was a believing scientist. In the book, he explains why he believes in God. I knew immediately I needed to read that book. That same afternoon I went to a secondhand bookstore and bought it. Now, I would not recommend it for theology but it fit me at the time.

Seeing a psychiatrist was kind of a threat. I did not know what they might conclude about me. After the tests and the interview, they tried to reassure me that my tests fit a missionary's profile. But, they added, "We cannot give you the results. We will send our report to the mission board and they will let you know."

I left wondering just what they would "let me know." On the way back to Iraan, I stopped in Dallas and consulted with my pastor, Dr. W. A. Welsh. His advice was, "Don't become a minister unless it becomes impossible for you to do anything else." Three months passed. I heard nothing from the mission board. I was debating: "Do I start my own company now, stay with the major company or become a missionary?" A fourth alternative was to quit thinking and take a leave of absence for a month in July and go to Europe, for the World's Fair in Brussels.

An agnostic engineer friend and I discussed flying to the Brussels World's Fair. He was a fine pilot, so we were considering chartering a plane. As we talked, this brilliant man asked questions for which I had no answers. Although I had always believed, now I began to doubt. In the past, I could believe without talking about it. If I were a missionary, talking about my faith would be my full-time work. I needed reassurance of my call and asked God, "One more time, let me know if you are real, and I will be a missionary."

Jesus spent 40 days in the wilderness before he began his ministry. I thought, "If Jesus could spend 40 days, I ought to be able to spend three; Friday night, Saturday and Sunday." So I asked a rancher friend in the church if I could go out on his ranch along the Pecos River. There would be no one within 50 square miles except one Mexican sheepherder, and he did not speak English. Since I didn't know Spanish, no one would bother my meditation and seeking.

It was early June of 1958. The Friday morning before I was to leave for the ranch, I received a letter from Joan. She was answering my Christmas card sent six months earlier. She said, "I've been in two Broadway shows. Now, I've been invited to represent the United States at the Brussels World's Fair, with leading roles in the musicals 'Carousel' and 'Wonderful Town.'"

She was excited because she would get to work with two very famous Broadway names: Richard Rodgers, who wrote "Carousel," and the famous choreographer, Agnes DeMille. I was excited too, and wrote her that morning saying, "This weekend I will decide whether to be a missionary or not. If not, I'll see you in Brussels next month."

After dropping the letter in the mail, I drove out about 75 miles to my friend's isolated ranch and set up a little camp. I began my vigil -- walking, sitting, praying, reading the Bible and, the book, *Human Destiny*. I was also looking, listening and hoping to see something like a burning bush, maybe a voice from Heaven or even a bolt of lightning. Nothing happened.

On Saturday afternoon, I saw the sheepherder down in the valley. In Acts 2 the first missionaries received the gift of tongues. They spoke, and other nationalities understood their message. I thought, "That's for me. I am an engineer. I don't like languages and never studied one. Lord! You just let me speak Spanish with that man, and I will know that I am supposed to be a missionary for sure."

I started down the hill. When I reached him, I smiled and tried to say something. There was no new language, but he did return my smile. In a spirit of friendliness, I exchanged some "22" rifle shells for matches, which I had forgotten to bring along. Then he went off to tend his sheep. I prayed, "Lord, I am not going to ask for any more miracles -- today. But I want you to take away my doubts that you are really here. I am going to pray all night until you do. I want to get this issue resolved." I prayed and prayed, but I couldn't stay awake. By ten o'clock, I fell asleep.

The next morning, I tried again. I read the Bible and *Human Destiny*. Basically, the author gave evidence to prove that it is far more rational and easier to believe that our infinitely

51

complex universe was formed by the Creator's mind than to believe everything came from an accident. I read, "Spiritual and moral truths have the only permanent and significant value." The words jumped off the page, and the gentle whisper said, "Where are your doubts now?" I rolled this around in my mind, and there were no more doubts! I knew that God was real, and I had to be a missionary. I had to devote my life to living and sharing spiritual and moral truths. I have never been able to find that exact sentence in the book again.

I closed the book, packed my things, and drove back to my office in the oilfield camp. There on my desk was the letter from the mission board for which I'd been waiting three months. It said, "Your tests are in order. Please report in two weeks to begin preparation for the mission field." It was a relief to know I was sane, but actually I had been planning to quit in August and begin my seminary study then. It was now only early June. However, I had made my decision that Sunday morning, and the letter came that afternoon. I resigned and flew to Indianapolis.

First, I was sent for an interview with a psychologist. She discussed the tests I had taken in Oklahoma three months earlier. She said, "You fit the pattern of missionaries, but I have one question from your tests. We cannot tell if you love your mother too much or not enough." I thought, "Who can answer that type of question? Too much or not enough love?" (See chap. 4, "Bitter Roots.") Then she went on to say, "We are wondering why you are not married. This does not keep you from mission candidacy, but the mission does not like to send single men overseas. They have not had good success in adjusting." I told her, "I certainly understand. I went to Korea as a single man, and I don't intend to go out single again. Since God has called me, I'm sure he will give me a wife."

COMING HOME

"No one can serve two masters. Either he will hate the one and love the other, or he will be devoted to the one and despise the other. You cannot serve both God and Money." Mt. 6:24

In Indianapolis, I visited all the different area offices. We discussed where in the world I might fit. I had no idea myself. Then I met Don West, the secretary for Southeast Asia. He introduced me to Dr. Douglas Corpron. Dr. Corpron said, "You are an engineer. We are planning to go up the Kwai River in western Thailand and open a hospital. You could come and build the hospital."

I had heard of the recent movie, "The Bridge Over the River Kwai," and I was interested. He gave me a report to read about the Talakone sect of the Karen tribe. That night, I propped up in bed and began to read. The report read something like this:

The Karen Tribe lives mostly in Burma, but there are many in Thailand too. When they were first contacted in Burma by missionaries in the early 1800s, the Karen responded in mass because of their legends. There are many versions of these stories, but, generally, for centuries they have believed that there was a Father God who created heaven, earth, sun and stars.

The Father God had created the Karen first, then the other races with the youngest brother being the white man. God gave them each a book to live by. Then he went away. All the brothers were scattered. The Karen did not take care of their book and allowed it to be destroyed when they were burning the mountainside to plant their rice. Since then, the Karen have been weak, oppressed, and poverty stricken. But the story goes on to say that some day the long lost white brother will come back to restore the "Golden Book" to the Karen, and so restore the good life.

The Talakone have their headquarters in Thailand near the Burma border. The Talakone were not ready when the first Karen evangelist came. They said, "Our 'white brother' will return during the reign of our seventh chief, whom we call 'Pujite.' Pujite means something like grandfather god. Recently, word has come out of the jungle that the seventh chief is now in power and wants to see the missionaries.

As I read that, I felt compelled to get up and kneel down beside the bed. It sounded wild and romantic, but, nevertheless, I felt I was to go to the Talakone. Four years later, we did make the first expedition to the Talakone. See the photos at the end of this book. The story will be in another book.

First, I had to decide where to study. I remembered when I was in the Army in New Orleans, I dated a girl who wanted to be a missionary. I told her, "You should go to Texas Christian University (TCU). You are more likely to find men from our denomination studying for the mission field there." I did not tell her I was interested in missions. As soon as I told her that, those words bounced back to me saying, "You are going to have to go to TCU to find a wife." Now, four years later, that thought returned as I was deciding where to study.

Without my telling anyone about this premonition, the mission executives recommended that I go to Brite College of the Bible (now Brite Divinity School) at Texas Christian University in Fort Worth, Texas. It was near my home in Dallas, and they wanted Prof. Bill Hall, the Missions Professor at Brite, to supervise my theological studies. Then I could go to Thailand as an engineer and help build the hospital.

I enrolled in July of 1958. That day was one of the most exciting days of my life. As I drove my little "Chevy" back home to Dallas, the car seemed to leap and skip. I shouted and sang. I may have spoken in tongues. I don't know, but I do know I was ecstatic. I was 28 years old and I finally knew why I was born.

The first course in Bible introduction was taught by Dr. James Moudy, my former student pastor at Texas A & M. It was like coming home. Every course was exciting. After about five months, while sitting in class, I heard that voice again, "You are going to be an evangelist," so I decided to finish the full 3-year course for a Master of Divinity. I would miss the opportunity to build the hospital, but I still felt called to Thailand.

As I took my first course in psychology, I remembered the question the psychologist in Indianapolis had raised of why I was not married. I had always thought that I had just not found the right girl. Now, I learned something about the Freudian concept, which teaches that the experiences of the first five years of a child's life determine the child's psychological problems later.

Dr. Charles Kemp was the Professor of Pastoral Care. I began weekly counseling sessions with him, trying to turn over those old rocks laid down in my past. I wanted to see what was buried there that might cause a psychological problem about getting married. I knew I needed a wife before going overseas.

Just before Christmas that year, I received a letter from Joan answering the letter I had written her the previous June. She said, "I did not see you in Brussels. I am coming down to Fort Worth from Broadway to play 'Laurie,' the leading female role in 'Oklahoma!' If you are anywhere around come see me." Not knowing where I was, she sent the letter to my parents' home in Dallas.

I was certainly around. TCU was about one mile from the Casa Manana Theater where Joan was scheduled to perform. I took the letter in to Dr. Kemp and said, "I know it sounds crazy, but I don't think I will need to see you any more. I think this is going to solve my problem."

Joan as "Laurie"in "Oklahoma!" - Casa Manana Theater, Ft. Worth, Texas (January. 1958)

Joan arrived just as I began my final exams. This was the first time I ever dared to try out the old adage, "If you study hard all semester, you won't have to study for finals." I had really studied, because I sincerely wanted to learn. This was different from my undergraduate days. It worked. I made all "A's" except for a "B" in Speech. I dated Joan every night after her rehearsals and dozed off during the Speech final.

Despite the finals, it was still a great week. I brought the whole cast of "Oklahoma!" to the seminary for the weekly Academic Guild luncheon with the Faculty and students. I did try, however, to be very cautious about our relationship. How could the mission field and show business meld? I did notice that Joan had gotten off the plane carrying *Fear and Trembling* by Kierkegaard. I knew this was a theology text for the "big boys" in the second year. Also, I could easily see she was a strong Christian.

By Saturday night, I could stand it no longer. I told her "I love you, Joan." "How much?" she asked, and I made the leap -. "Enough to marry you."

It took her two weeks to say, "Yes" because she was semi-engaged. Joan still had to complete a nine-month contract with Richard Rodgers, for a road show revival of the first show that had made Mr. Rogers famous, "Babes in Arms." I flew to New York to negotiate with her agent about her contract. He said, "Joan is such a natural. Only something like mission work could take her out of show business. She has 'It.'"

Besides me, of course, there was another reason why Joan was able to leave a promising career behind her. While in Hollywood, she had attended the Hollywood Presbyterian Church where she heard Dr. Harold Linquist preach from Matthew 6:24, "No one can serve two masters. ...You cannot serve both God and Money." Actually, she was not so interested in money. She wanted her name in lights on Broadway, because for her that was the epitome of theatrical success. She was getting there.

The previous year, 1958, Joan had been selected for the Theatre World Award as one of the ten most "Promising Personalities" on Broadway. She had also just finished a very successful Alcoa Hour TV special with Roddy McDowell. She was headed for the top, but God had a different plan.

The next nine long months dragged by while Joan completed her singing and acting contract. Finally, on December 12, 1959, we were married in the Chapelwood Methodist Church, Joan's home church in Houston. Rev. Grady Hardin, her former pastor, performed the ceremony. He wasn't a stranger to me because I had been his host years before when he came to Texas A & M for a Religious Emphasis Week.

Publicity shot of Mary Martin lending Joan her fur coat for the revival of "Leave it to Me" in Dallas, Texas. (Fall, 1959) This was Joan's last show.

Just married – December 12, 1959

Joan and I enjoyed our mission studies together, and David Allan added to our joy when he arrived the end of September, 1960.

The next two years flew by. In June of 1961 we were both ordained in East Dallas Christian Church and left for Thailand in August. As we flew in over the green rice fields and approached the landing field in Bangkok, I told Joan, "I feel like we are coming home." She said, "That is exactly how I feel, too."

Home in Bangkok (1961)

Now, after 42 years, we still feel the same way.
We are home! In Chiang Mai

CHAPTER 3

FORGIVE MY SINS

"Forgive us our sins..." Luke 11:4

"Cleanse me with hyssop, and I will be clean; wash me, and I will be whiter than snow." Ps. 51:7

HELP ME CHANGE MY LIFE

"Therefore, if anyone is in Christ, he is a new creation; the old has gone, the new has come!" 2 Cor. 5:17

Lamut's village was known as a place where you could hire a gunman. It was said that only policemen who were connected with the local gangs dared to go into the village. After Lamut became a Christian he took me there, and it seemed as though I had a glimpse of hell. Everywhere people were talking about stealing, revenge, and murder. Several young men were lounging on the bridge as we crossed into the village. Lamut nodded toward the men and said, "They are the new generation of gunmen, just waiting to make a name for themselves."

Within a month of that visit, a doctor was shot off his motorcycle on the road near our home, but he was able to kill the gunman. Lamut told me the dead man was one of those inexperienced young men we had seen on the bridge that night. He had been hired to shoot the doctor, because the doctor had taken another man's girlfriend. The gunman hid in the ditch and shot the doctor, who fell in the ditch on the other side of the road. When the "greenhorn" stood up to finish the job, the wounded doctor pulled out his pistol and killed the gunman.

In those days it seemed as though everyone traveled armed except the head teacher and me. Customarily, when a man went out, he tucked a pistol or a knife in his belt behind his back. It was hidden under his shirt, but he had easy access because the shirt was hanging loose. Lamut told me that even when he was in the army, they used army weapons to make raids at night. The next morning, they went back to being good soldiers.

Lamut bought land and moved into our area near the Lao Song tribal village of Lamkrajao where we were working. He was trying to get away from the influence of old his gangster village and make a new start. We first heard about him after someone tried to break into his bamboo home and steal his bicycle. He had shot it out with them, but they got away in the dark.

Lamut first heard the gospel when a Lao Song lady near his home told him about the change in her brother. Her brother had admitted to killing two men but was now a new and better person after becoming a Christian. Lamut was interested and wanted to change also because he was worried about all his sins. He thought he could change by himself by doing good to make up for all his bad deeds. He sought to do this through his own folk religious understanding.

In Lamut's understanding there was no way to escape from paying for past evil conduct. However, one could earn merit to offset the wrong. Lamut decided to make merit by organizing a group in the Lamkrajao area to give money and take gifts to help the annual religious fair in his old home village.

He also helped sponsor a "dime-a-dance" to earn money for the fair and merit for himself. Usually men would not get up on the stage to dance until they had a few drinks for courage. Lamut and his friends were drinking, even though drinking was a violation of their religious code. He said, "The drinks led to a quarrel when my old buddies began to razz me. They said, 'Look at you. You've lost your touch with the ladies.'" Lamut already had three wives, but their taunts were still a threat to his manhood. He lost his temper and drew his gun.

He told me later, "One rule I live by is, 'I never draw my gun without pulling the trigger.' If you don't shoot first, the other person will shoot you. But for some reason, I couldn't pull the trigger. As I stood there with my gun in my hand, I realized I was incapable of changing by myself. Here I was, the leader of this festival to make merit and to turn over a new leaf in life. Yet, I was about to kill someone at the fair. I gave the gun away and left."

Lamut continued, "I came to see you because I know now that I can't change by myself. I heard that Jesus can help a person change, and I want Jesus to help me. I want to be a Christian." We led him in a prayer to receive Jesus as Lord and Savior, to ask Jesus to forgive his sins, and to lead him into new life. Lamut came to church the next Sunday and made a confession of faith.

That Sunday, Lamut said, "Now, I am getting a good night's sleep." Then he explained why. Lamut had many enemies. The favorite way to get rid of your enemies was to sneak up at night and shoot them through the thin bamboo walls, killing them while they slept. Or, if they slept in a raised house, they could be shot through the floor. For years, each night Lamut had blown out his little kerosene lamp and slipped out of the house to sleep in the fields where no one could find him. Now Lamut put his trust in Christ and slept in his own bed. "If I die, I die, he said. "I am in God's hands."

Then one Sunday, he declared, "I have quit smoking and drinking." He had found the power spoken about in I Corinthians 6:12, and said he would not be a slave to anything. Actually, we had not even mentioned smoking and drinking, because we were much more concerned about his robbing and killing. For instance, he told us that he had been seeking revenge on the men who had tried to break in his house and steal his bicycle when he first moved into our area. Lamut felt he had to keep up his reputation, so he couldn't let those thieves treat him like that. For two years he had been tracking them. He learned that there were two men, and he found out who they were. He intended to kill them so no one would dare bother him like that again.

Before he was able to take any action, someone else killed one of them. Then one night he saw the other one dancing on a "dime-a-dance" stage. Lamut sent his buddy up to cut in, planning to hide in the shadows and shoot the man once he was separated from the girl. However, before his buddy could cut in, a fight broke out, and Lamut could not tell who to shoot.

He devised another plan, thinking, "This man is a well-known thief and always carries a gun. He doesn't know that I know he tried to steal my bicycle. I'll be friendly and invite him to my house. Then I will shoot him, fire his gun a couple of times, and claim self defense."

By now Lamut was a baptized Christian. One day, unexpected and uninvited, his enemy walked into Lamut's house. Lamut said, "I stood shocked for a moment thinking what to do. Then I turned, fixed the thief a meal and served him. As we ate together the man confessed his attempted theft, and we were no longer enemies." In fact, it was Lamut who later took his former enemy to the hospital for treatment when someone else shot him down along the road.

Before Lamut was baptized, the Sam Yaek church board met to decide about Lamut's three wives. During the meeting, I told them a story I had heard during missionary orientation before I came to the mission field. The story goes back 100 years. An African chief came to a missionary and wanted to be baptized. The missionary asked him how many wives he had. The chief told him that he had 100. The missionary said, "When you only have one wife left, come back and I will baptize you."

From time to time the missionary saw the chief and asked him if he was ready. The chief would reply, "Not yet!" Finally, after two years, the chief came. He said, "Now I am ready for baptism." The missionary asked him, "Why has it taken so long?" The chief said, "It wasn't easy to get rid of the other 99 wives." The missionary asked, "Why was that?" The chief replied, "I can't eat that fast." I told the board that this story must be apocryphal. They all laughed, but they got the point.

After some discussion, it was decided that it was not right to invite only one wife to be baptized and not let the other two be saved as well. The church would let them all be baptized, but Lamut could not become an elder or deacon with three wives, nor could he take more wives. The discussion was academic, however, because two of his wives left Lamut before he could be baptized, and the remaining wife wanted to wait.

After Lamut's baptism, we all went out to his house. He dedicated his land to Christ's care, and gave up worshiping the spirits of the land. This took a tremendous amount of faith and courage, because the neighbors said, "You wait, the spirits will get you for this." Sure enough, the first year he had a crop failure. This made Lamut a little worried about the spirits until he looked around. The bugs and drought had affected other people's crops as well as his even though the others still cared for the spirits.

We took a Christian agriculturist out to talk with him. Lamut found that he could sell banana leaves to use for wrapping meat in the market. Also there was a tree in his field, which produced fruit he could sell.

One day he proudly announced, "See those chickens? I have never been able to have chickens to sell before. When the gang used to get together here to plan a job, we'd have a few drinks and then we'd have to boil a chicken to go with the drinks. Now that I've quit the gang and quit drinking, I have a hundred chickens to sell."

Anong, Lamut's last wife, waited five years to be baptized. By then we had moved to Chiang Mai. Anong came north to a women's meeting. She told me, "I was waiting to see if Lamut actually could change. I have been baptized, and now I really know what it is to be born again."

Lamut and Anong (2002)

LAMUT'S NEW EYES

"So from now on we regard no one from a worldly point of view. Though we once regarded Christ in this way, we do so no longer."2 Cor. 5:16

Lamut used to regard others from a worldly or human point of view. If others were not directly helping him, they were just competitors to be beaten, tools to be manipulated, or threats to be annihilated. Now he had "new eyes" to see things from God's point of view.

He was so excited by the change in his own life that he began to look around and see others who needed this "Good news." Soon he brought six for baptism. Three of these were hoodlums like himself, the most colorful being the Mother Tiger of Lovely Valley. Another was the Mother Tiger's gunman, Nai Hawm. (See chap 1, "Keep the Birds out of My Field.")

With his "new eyes," Lamut not only found a way to care for his own family in time of drought, but he brought two landless families to live on his own land, and eat from his own kitchen. He soon found that helping people is not easy. He had built a house for one of the poor families to live next to him. The man had been his friend, but when I went out to see Lamut one night he was very angry with his new neighbor. He said they hadn't spoken in days because his former friend was now taking advantage of him and claiming that land to be his own.

I didn't know what to do, so I said, "Let's pray." After prayer, I said to Lamut, "If I go next door and talk to him, will you follow me over there and speak to him so that we can begin to work out this misunderstanding?" I was somewhat surprised when Lamut said he would. I went next door and talked to the neighbor about the problem.

The neighbor told me he didn't intend to claim that land, and that he wanted to be reconciled. Just when I got to that point Lamut came in the door. It was a big relief to me, because I wasn't sure that he would really come. I explained both of their positions again in their presence, and they agreed it was a misunderstanding. I felt their friendship was restored. Later the neighbor was able to find a small piece of land, and move to his own place.

Lamut saw that his Lao Song neighbors were losing their land because of high interest rates on the loans they had to take out. Some were moving to the jungle and coming under communist influence. Lamut pushed the church to help. We did help in lending rice, starting a handicraft project, and bringing in agricultural experts, but this was not enough.

Lamut turned to the Thai government. There was a USAID program available to start farmers' co-ops, which would supply pumps for water, insecticide, good seed and fertilizer. The catch was to find enough members to qualify. The government officials told Lamut that they would have to put the Lao Song village and the nearby Thai village together in one co-op. When he told the villagers, they just laughed. It had not been long before this that these two ethnic groups had met each other in the fields between the villages with hoes and clubs to fight over land boundaries. Even now, they hardly dared go into each other's village after dark.

Another obstacle was Lamut's past. At one time Lamut had been on the provincial "most wanted" list. Our area had developed so much that the government decided to make it a sub-district headquarters. The policeman who had formerly been assigned to catch Lamut was now our new sub-district chief. Amazingly, the previous year USAID had taken the chief to visit the United States to look at U.S. police methods. There he had met a black Christian policeman, who took him into his own home and treated him so well that the chief was touched. Now, when he moved into this new assignment, the chief could see the changes in Lamut. Because of his experience with Christians in the United States, he trusted and supported Lamut in these development projects.

Lamut was still scoffed at, gossiped about and, worst of all, he was laughed at. Previously he had been the least trusted man of the whole area, but now with his tremendous energy harnessed by Christ, he set out to make the co-op happen. He lived between the Thai and Lao Song villages, and he felt that with God's help he could bring reconciliation. He won the confidence of the villagers and the government officials. The co-op dream became a reality, and Lamut was elected the first president.

He still struggled every day to keep the old life from coming back. Lamut would come peddling up to our house saying, "Quick! Pray for me before the rage takes over." He said, "If I miss church just two Sundays in a row, I can feel the power of the devil getting stronger." When a local thug tested Lamut about "turning the other cheek," Lamut said, "I knew right then it was either go for the church or go for my gun."

To pay back a loan, one of the Lao Song families had given about one-half acre of land for a church. First we had built a small wooden house to use as a handicraft center. Lamut moved his family in to become the on-site coordinator for the Lao Song handicraft project which had expanded to several nearby villages.

One day I heard from a Lao Song lady that all the villagers were ready to drive Lamut out. At a handicraft meeting he had slapped Nai Kam, one of the new Christian Lao Song men. As she put it, "Once the glass has been broken, it is impossible to put it back together." Feeling my usual helplessness, I drove out to see Lamut and ask him what happened. He said, "That blankety blank accused me in front of all the other people, saying that I had stolen from the Lao Song handicraft funds, and I lost my temper!"

I was very conscious that Lamut was Thai and, therefore, an outsider. All the others were Lao Song. Again, I said, "Let's pray." Then I felt led to ask, "If I go and talk to Nai Kam first, will you go with me to see him and raise your hands in a 'wai' to show your apology and regret?" He nodded agreement.

With the picture of the "broken glass" in my mind and prayers in my heart, I went to see Nai Kam. I told him, "Lamut is sorry and wants to be forgiven. Will you please accept your part of the responsibility? If someone publicly accused you of stealing you know you would be angry also." He sort of nodded and I took this for agreement. When I brought Lamut, he "waied." This was the beginning of reconciliation, which grew until they could continue to work and worship together.

With Lamut's new heart came new eyes to help him discern right and wrong. This is illustrated in one of the most effective tracts that I have seen used with villagers. It is known as the "Heart Tract."

One picture shows a black heart with different animals inside. There is a dog, which represents stealing; a snake to represent lying and cheating; a tiger for anger, revenge and killing; a turtle for laziness; a pig for greed and filth; a goat for stubbornness; and a peacock for pride. In the center is a green demon putting out an eye with his spear to show that when you allow all these sins to work in you, you finally are unable to see what is right and wrong. There is also a mouth that is sealed. Whenever we explain that to villagers they nod, laugh and agree, "We have those."

The white heart picture shows the dove of the Spirit and the Bible as the Word coming into the heart, chasing the animals and the demon out. The heart is bright and shining. The eye is wide open and the mouth is sharing the joy of new life.

Achan Yongute Kampira explains the black and white hearts at a Thai folk drama evangelistic performance

Lamut said that tract really fit him. He gave an example of not being able to see what was right and wrong. He said, "Before I knew Jesus Christ, I took pride in my thievery. One of my proudest nights was when I saw a man pole-fishing beside the canal. His boat was tied some distance away. I quietly slunk and slithered through the grass. I cut the rope on the boat with my knife and soundlessly climbed in. Then I paddled the boat right in front of the fisherman. I spoke to him as I stole his boat and paddled away thinking, 'Look what I can do!' Now since Jesus has given me new eyes, I am ashamed of what I used to boast about."

Pa Yu (left), the Christian Lao Song lady who shared the
gospel with Lamut

DON'T GIVE UP ON LAMUT

"How can I give you up, Ephraim?...For I am God, and not man ..." Hosea 11:8-9

After Lamut left the gang and became a Christian, he was one of the church's prized examples because of his strong testimony and the obvious change in his life. There was, however, always a little nagging feeling that he might fall back into his old ways. In the New Testament, people were baptized immediately upon their declaration of faith. Not only Jews who had a background of faith in God, but also the Ethiopian eunuch and the Philippian jailer. The jailer and his whole family were immediately baptized when they declared their faith in Jesus Christ.

It is understandable why the church gradually put restrictions on new believers, requiring more instruction before baptism. In Sam Yaek we felt, although we did not say it publicly, that as long as new believers were not baptized, the church was not fully responsible. Thus, there would be no embarrassment if someone fell away. However, if they fell after baptism, the church would suffer great loss of face.

We had baptized Lamut and now were responsible. I went away on a trip. When I returned I did not see Lamut in church and asked where he was. After some hesitant looks, I was told that he had gone back to his old home place, the center for gangs of robbers and hired killers. Now, he was selling heroin. Heroin! My reaction was immediate anger, and I wanted to dismiss him to reap the fruit of what he was sowing.

Often God speaks to us with a gentle whisper or still small voice, the way he must have spoken to Elijah in 2 Kings 19:12-13. Sometimes he tells us things we don't want to do, and the whisper is so gentle that we brush it aside. If it is God's voice it will keep returning, and deep in our hearts we will know it is telling us what we must do. Now I heard that whisper, "Don't give up on Lamut."

That prodding gentle whisper kept coming back saying, "You must go and see Lamut." I tried to answer the voice with, "What's the use? It's too late now. How can he come back after selling heroin? Let him get what he deserves." But the whisper kept returning. Finally, after a month, I decided to go and see him even if it would do no good. I was his pastor. It was my duty to make the effort.

It was a 40-mile drive to Ban Kaem village where Lamut lived. His mother told me that he was not there but was out in their house in the rice fields. She pointed across the water. The whole area was flooded as far as the eye could see. Far out in the expanse of water were three little brown shapes that could just be detected as houses.

"Do I have to wade through all that water on such a hopeless mission?" Nevertheless, I began rolling up my pant legs and took off my shoes. Having come this far, I might as well go all the way. Thinking about sharp snail shells, leeches and snakes, I said a prayer while putting my feet into the water-covered mud. It was only about knee deep, but it took quite a while to wade the half mile or so. What could one say to make any difference to Lamut? I could only say out loud, "Well Lord, I'm doing this, even though I know it won't do any good. But if that whisper is really you, then maybe something good can happen."

When I approached the house, raised on poles above the water, Lamut appeared at the ladder and invited me to climb up. Feeling very inadequate, I sat down on the floor. His wife, Anong, gave me a cup of water. After thanking her, I did not know what else to say except that I felt God had sent me to see them. They said nothing. After a few awkward attempts met by long silences, I asked if I could say a prayer. Lamut nodded, and I prayed for a blessing on them. Then I got up and made the long trek back to the Land Rover and on back to Sam Yaek, feeling very weak and unfulfilled.

After a month, Lamut and Anong suddenly appeared. They had moved back to their home in Lamkrajao near us and had quit the heroin trade. He once more became active in the church and helped coordinate the handicraft project in the Lao Song villages.

Lao Song handicraft project

About a year later our family moved to Chiang Mai to teach in the seminary. Lamut worked for 20 years with the Christian Lao Song handicraft project. Then I heard that he had retired and moved south to Ban Kha, Ratchaburi Province, where his son had homesteaded land in the jungle. Later on, I received two messages that Lamut wanted me to come and help him start a church.

"How can I help start a church way down in that remote corner of Ratchaburi?" I thought. "I could never stay long enough to help very much. Again that gentle whisper came, "You have to go see Lamut." Finally, after two years, I called Achan Kasem Treintong. He was a Lao Song from Lamkrajao, who had come to our school at Sam Yaek, and became one of the first two Christians from his village. We had helped him to get a scholarship to study for his master's degree in Texas. Now he was head of all the Christian schools belonging to the Church of Christ in Thailand. Achan Kasem was always ready to help in evangelism, and he would visit Christian schools on his way. We set a date to drive the 600 miles south and visit Lamut.

In August, 1996, the day before we were to leave, I received a call from my sister, Margaret, in Dallas, asking me to come home because our mother had just died in her sleep. She was 97 years old. I cancelled my trip and flew home.

Eight months went by. Kasem, Joan and I set another date to visit Lamut. We went first to Sam Yaek, where I was to preach for the Baccalaureate of the school in March of 1997. During the night we received an urgent call that our daughter, Ruthanne, her husband and three-year-old son were critically injured in an accident in northeast Thailand. We drove to the hospital and stayed a week, praying and asking for the Lord's intervention, but our grandson died. Ruthanne and her husband, Oot, gradually recovered. More about this tragedy is told in chapter 6, " The Death of a Grandson."

Once again, I did not get to see Lamut. The whisper inside still prodded, and I began to feel that I could not let any obstacle keep me from getting there. I made a date in March 1999 with Achan Bamrung, my old friend who had pioneered in establishing the Sam Yaek school. He was 83 and long retired, but still active and ready to help. The moderator and her husband of the Lamkrajao Lao Song Church, where Lamut had lived and worked with the handicraft for 20 years, agreed to drive us. Kasem and Joan were not free. This time we found our way in to see Lamut without incident.

He was thrilled and showed us two possible locations he had chosen for a church. We prayed and shared old times. It was Saturday and, because of church responsibilities, we could only stay a few hours. As we drove back, I thought, "Well Lord, we did it, but I don't see how much can come of it. It is so far from all of us." Again, I was mistaken. Sometime later I learned that Achan Bamrung shared Lamut's Macedonian call with the Sam Yaek Church and the church district. They had all agreed to make the establishment of a church in Lamut's area a priority project. The Sam Yaek Church people began to make evangelistic visits and worship there one Saturday each month.

In March of 2001, the CCI Folk Drama Troupe performed in Lamut's area. Joan and I were invited to dinner at Lamut's home. Lamut and Anong said again, as they had many times through the years, "We will never forget how we felt when we saw you wading through the muddy water coming to see us. We knew God had not given up on us."

Ban Kha Chapel (2001)

The new chapel at Ban Kha was built on 10 rai of land (about five acres) given by Lamut and his family. It is located on a hillside overlooking a beautiful valley and was dedicated in May 2001. Achan Bamrung baptized a former hired killer and Lamut's grandson as part of the dedication service. The grandson is now chairman of the church board, and the former assassin's sister is taking instruction for baptism.

A few days before this was written we visited her, and she said, "None of us believed that my brother could change. Now he is a different man, and I want righteousness too."

Nai Phet and Lamut's grandson, Samakhom, prepare for baptism on dedication day. (2001)

Achan Bamrung baptizing Nai Phet,
the gunman, at the dedication.

THE MOTHER TIGER OF LOVELY VALLEY

"Do not take revenge, my friends, but leave room for God's wrath, for it is written: 'It is mine to avenge; I will repay,' says the Lord." Rom. 12:19

When we first met Mother Tiger, she had two guns tucked in her sarong. She and her 28-year-old daughter had just gotten out of jail for armed robbery. There was not enough evidence for a trial, but they were kept in jail longer because the daughter beat up the policeman when they were arrested.

Mother Tiger and her daughter had opened a little store in the new village of Lovely Valley. When they came back they found their store empty. While they were in jail, the village headman thought the two women would be put away for some time, so he let his men clean out their store.

When Mother Tiger returned and found the store empty, she felt she had two choices: kill the headman or move away, and she did not intend to move. She hesitated to kill the headman, because she would be caught in an endless cycle of revenge. If she killed the headman, his son would have to kill her. That meant she would have to kill the son before he killed her, and it would go on and on...

Lamut, the former ex-hoodlum, came and said, "Look, there's a new way. You can give your old life to Jesus and start a new one. Let God take care of the headman." She was interested and agreed to hear more. Lamut took Achan Bamrung, the head teacher, and me to visit. Achan Bamrung used a picture roll of the life of Christ to tell of Jesus' birth, his miracles, message, death and resurrection.

As she listened to the simple gospel story that night, Mother Tiger's face softened, and she became more relaxed.

She agreed to let us pick her up for church the next Sunday. As soon as we reached the church, she found a seat on the back row. At the close of the service, we sang our usual invitation hymn, "Just as I Am." To our surprise, Mother Tiger came walking down the aisle just as she was.

I knew that Mother Tiger wore a very expensive magic charm made from the forehead of a tiger. It was especially valuable to gangsters because it was supposed to make "bullets bounce off and knives not cut."

When the hymn was over, I whispered to her, "We are glad that you have come forward to receive Jesus, but if you really believe, you must take off that charm." Amazingly, she took it right off. She passed the first test so I whispered again. "Mae (Mother), If you are going to be Christian, you can't kill the headman."

She boomed out, "Oh! I'm not gonna kill him. That's why I came down to the front. I'm gonna let my daughter do it."

These stories can be told in a short time, but a changed life is a long struggle. We dropped the "Tiger" title and called her by her real name - Aunt See. We also had to find a new occupation for her. The old one wouldn't do. Joan taught Aunt and her daughter to sew Christmas angels that could be sold to the Christian ladies in Bangkok. One day I drove out to see her. As I ducked my head to come in the door of her bamboo house, the mother and daughter were sewing. Mother looked up and greeted me in her old loud hard voice, "I'm still gonna get revenge on that headman." My heart missed a beat. She continued, "I'm praying for him that he becomes Christian."

When I reflect about how Mother Tiger's laughter softened, and her face and demeanor changed when the head teacher first showed her the picture roll and told her the gospel story, I must confess that the power of the gospel is still a mystery to me. I do not fully understand, even though I have spent much of my life trying. However, I have seen that when we share the gospel and trust, it is the power of God for salvation, and it changes lives.

I must also admit that we became a little hesitant to sing that invitation hymn, because we did not know who was going to come forward next. We were tired of the struggle. We really wanted those "good people" to join our church—those with plenty of money and no problems. But Jesus calls sinners to come just as they are.

Mother Tiger (Aunt See) with daughter, Kruawan before baptism. (1965)

Baptism at Sam Yaek Church (Christmas, 1966) From left front Aunt See, Lao Song lady, Achan Bamrung. Allan in back.

Mae Claeow led us into a village to hold a Bible study
with people who had killed the first two Christians.

A WEEKEND WITH MAE CLAEOW

"...I am sending you to open their eyes and turn them from darkness to light, and from the power of Satan to God, so that they may receive forgiveness of sins and a place among those who are sanctified by faith in me." Acts 26:17b-18.

Mae (mother) Claeow Krailuet is one of the most remarkable people I have ever met. Everyone called her "Mae Claeow" In 1964, Joan and I were invited to hold a series of meetings at the Christian women's academy in Trang. It was a city about 500 miles south of Nakhon Pathom, where we lived. During the week we were invited to visit the evangelism points started by Mae Claeow.

Mae Claeow was a Bible woman, supporting herself by walking through the rubber plantations and jungle selling Bible portions at 25 satang each. At that time 25 satang was equivalent to about one cent. We prepared to go with Mae on Saturday morning. Two other women joined us for the trip. They were called the "the three musketeers," and they worked all week to earn money to pay for these evangelism weekends. We rented two motorcycles with built-on extensions so that four could ride on one motorcycle.

Three musketeers – Mae Claeow, center

The motorcycles could only go part way to the first place we were to visit. We had to walk about an hour to hold an afternoon meeting with a small group of new believers. Mae told us that the first two who became Christian had been killed. It was common knowledge who had committed the murders. The police, who visited this lawless area occasionally, said they lacked enough evidence to arrest them.

One of the killers had already confessed faith in Jesus and was in the meeting that afternoon, while the second was watching not far away. After the meeting, we walked back and were picked up to go to the second village to spend the night.

In the village, Mae led us out for visitation in homes. Joan and I did not feel very competent even in the Central Thai dialect, and the dialect in the south was quite different. When Joan asked what she should do, Mae told her, "Just read a scripture, the Word of God has power of its own." Joan and I did this. We felt we had done our best and could trust God for the results.

That night before the meeting, the owner of the house where we stayed told us his story of faith. He said that about ten years before, his wife had fallen ill and he was sure she would die. He decided to go into the city of Trang to buy medicine and her favorite food. He had lost hope that his wife would get well, and wanted to give her one last good meal. When he entered the market he heard people telling of the foreign preacher who was praying for people at the Christian church, and they were being healed. (See chap. 7, "Laying on Hands"). He went back to his village and took his wife in an oxcart out to the main road. Then they caught a bus back to Trang.

They went to the packed churchyard and stayed there for three days until the preacher, Brother T. L. Osborne, from Oklahoma came to them and prayed for his wife. She got up, walked to the bus and went back healed to her village. They stopped worshiping the spirits and worshiped God in Jesus Christ. For two years, they were the only believers in the area. Then the husband heard there was a "Jesus woman" selling scriptures nearby. He ran and brought her to his home, and now they have been holding Christian meetings for almost a year. I thought of how many times I had heard older missionaries complain, "That Oklahoma healer just stirred up trouble."

People gathered in the little bamboo worship pavilion next to the house. Mae asked me to preach. All I could do was pray and try to use my poor language as best I could. I spoke about the power of the resurrected Christ. When I finished, I started to sit down, but Mae said, "Give an invitation!" So I stood up and asked anyone who wanted to receive salvation through Jesus Christ to walk forward. I was amazed to see 14 men, heads of non-Christian families, walk forward, declare their faith and pray to receive Jesus as Lord and Savior.

The next day we went to another village to meet with about six believers in a small store. On the way into the village, we passed men building a bridge to get ready for the wet season. We stopped, and Mae introduced us to the man who was directing the construction and working the hardest. He was the village headman. He apologized for not coming to the meeting but said he had to finish the bridge.

As we left, Mae told me about him. She said,

He was not the headman before, but a robber and a thug. He came to hear me preach as I sold the scriptures here the first time. Later he told me that he saw I was by myself and must have money from selling things. He planned to waylay me on the trail back. When I passed by, for some unknown reason he just let me go.

Because some people here were very interested on the first visit, I returned a second time and showed a picture roll about the power of the Gospel. The robber came again. This time he said he was determined not to let me get away, but by the time I finished preaching he had been pierced to the heart. He came to me to accept Jesus and his life was changed. Previously, he had only lived to take advantage of others, but now he started to help. The villagers saw the change and began to trust him. They could see his ability. At election time he was chosen to be headman.

On another occasion when we went down to work with Mae she seemed very disturbed. She said a group of western missionaries had come to offer help in supporting and nurturing the churches she had planted. They explained to her that it was unscriptural for a woman to preach, and she would have to stop. She said to us, "If God doesn't want me to preach, how did these five churches grow up? I can't deny my call and I have sent word to the churches not to receive these men."

Several years later a lovely church was built. We drove down from Chiang Mai with our Folk Drama Troupe. At that time the area was filled with communist terrorists. Mae had built a stage in front of the church. As the performance began, Mae came and told me that I should stay behind the backdrops. She said, "There are more than 20 guerillas in the audience, and they don't like white faces." I was glad to keep out of sight and pray. We sold all of our scripture portions that night. Later Mae sent word that five of those young communists became believers.

FIGHTING A PYTHON

"And these signs will accompany those who believe: In my name... they will pick up snakes with their hands; and when they drink deadly poison, it will not hurt them at all..."
Mk. 16:17-18

One afternoon Mae Claeow was walking back through the jungle from a village where she had been selling her scripture portions. The sky darkened, and there was so much thunder and lightning that she hurried her walk, trying to reach the road before the rain began. Suddenly, a tremendous bolt of lightning struck a huge tree ahead, and it came crashing down across the trail. When Mae came to the tree, she had to climb up and over. Climbing down on the other side, she stepped on a large branch sticking out from the trunk.

As she stepped on it, the branch moved, and she was filled with fear. It was not a branch at all, but a very large python whose head had been caught under the tree when it fell. The snake was still very much alive and immediately wrapped its tail around Mae's leg. Her shoulder bag of books went flying in the air. She began to claw desperately at the muddy ground to keep the python from pulling her under the tree and wrapping more coils around her. She fought and stretched the python out away from the tree. Then the snake's strength would pull her back again. This happened over and over again. It was a life and death struggle.

Just as she felt she had no more strength to resist, she saw a short stick beside her on the ground. She grasped up the stick and placed it by the tip of the tail that was waving around her leg. Amazingly, the snake began to wrap around the stick. It released her leg, coiling into a big writhing mass under the tree. She crawled away and collapsed in the mud.

A farmer came hurrying along the trail, trying to get home out of the rain. He had a big machete in his hands. When he saw this muddy, disheveled woman dressed in black, with her long black hair stringing down around her face, he backed away in fright. He raised his machete high over his head in defense. Shaking and stammering, he demanded, "Who are you?" He thought Mae was a spirit.

She could not speak, but pointed to the huge snake under the tree. The farmer then helped her pick up her scattered books and led her on the trail to the road. She still could not speak when she boarded a bus. Mae gestured to the driver to get off at the home of a Christian friend on the way back to Trang. She knocked on the door and saw the look of horror on her friend's face when she opened the door. Mae still could not speak and had to use sign language. Her friend helped her to get a bath and put her to bed.

She slept fitfully, almost in a coma, for three days. Her friend watched her as she slept. Later, she told Mae, "You would sit up and then pull back on the bars at the foot of the bed with all your might. It was as if you were still struggling to escape the coils of the snake." On the third day, Mae woke up and could speak. She got up, dressed, ate, and went home to Trang. After another week, she was back out in the jungle selling her scriptures.

Mae told me on a later occasion, that she had been fed poison. It felt like red ants biting her throat all the way down to her stomach, but she was able to get up and get away. She also told me, "Once I walked right beside a sleeping tiger before I realized it. The tiger never moved."

THE ROOM FILLED WITH STARS

**"Rejoice in the Lord always. I will say it again: Rejoice!"
Phil. 4:4**

As we traveled to visit the new believers, Mae Claeow shared how she came to believe.

I was not a very good woman and had a bad temper. I had become the minor wife of a Chinese businessman in Phuket on the Andaman Sea. Once I was so angry with my mother-in-law that I put poison in her food, but she did not die. Later my husband took a third wife, and I went into an inner rage.

One night, I dressed in black, covered my face and went to the home of the middleman who arranged the new marriage. I knocked on the door. When the man came to the door, I swung my machete as hard as I could and hit him between the eyes. He screamed, and I ran and hid in the bushes, watching to see what would happen. He cried out with blood flowing down his face, and people came running to help. They called an ambulance and took him off. I was disappointed when he did not die. No one ever suspected that I was the one who hit him.

A friend invited me to church saying God could help me still my rage. I went with her, and it was true. I felt peace while I was in church, and it lasted even when I went home.

I made a trip to see relatives and missed a train connection in a very remote place. Then, somehow, I lost my money purse too. I had to wait all night in a lonely and dangerous area. The next day when the train came, I prayed. "Lord God, I have no money. If you are God let me get on the train and get safely to my relatives." I boarded the train and sat down. The conductor passed by several times collecting tickets but never even looked at me. I knew then that God is real.

Sometime later, I attended a revival. I declared my faith and was baptized. I asked the pastor if I could stay in the church and pray for several days after the revival closed. I slept on the floor and prayed to be able to read the Bible so I could tell all my relatives the good news. I had been to school briefly when I was little but could never read. Seven days passed.

On the seventh day I was lying on my back, clutching my Bible to my chest, when slowly the church room filled with stars. The stars were very big, and they gradually came down just above my face. There was Thai writing on them, and I could understand it. One said Matthew. Another said, Mark. Another, Luke, and so on.

Just then the pastor called to me because I had not come out to eat all day. As I walked to the door, I opened my Bible and read Philippians 4:4 out loud, 'Rejoice in the Lord, and again I say rejoice!' Praise God, I could read.

How can we believe such a seemingly wild story? Joan and I watched her life. We helped her as much as we could for more than 30 years before she died. We saw her honesty, mature wisdom, dedication, and accomplishment as she lived out her life. She was never able to read any other writing but the Bible.

Mae Claeow served for 40 years selling scriptures and planting churches. The Thai Prime Minister gave her an award for her service to society. She has been an outstanding example in evangelism and church nurture. Seven churches grew from her ministry. Mae Claeow died January 30, 1997, at the age of 87.

Her dedicated service continues to bear fruit. She deserves an honored place in the history of the Thai church.

Two of Mae Claeow's new Christians. The man was epileptic and unable to speak but was healed through prayer

Some of the heads of families who came forward at our invitation and began the church at Kokmueang. (1964)

Kokmueang Church, Yan Ta Khao District, Trang Province, (1968) One of the seven churches Mae Claeow founded - Mae Claeow far left front. (See "A Weekend with Mae Claeow")

CHAPTER 4

DELIVER US FROM EVIL

POWERS AND PRINCIPALITIES - Background

"Put on the full armor of God so that you can take your stand against the devil's schemes. For our struggle is not against flesh and blood, but against the rulers, against the authorities, against the powers of this dark world and against the spiritual forces of evil in the heavenly realms." Eph. 6:11-12

The stories in this chapter about the powers and principalities may seem very strange, even unbelievable to many readers. Westerners, including most of my friends, have been steeped in psychological analysis, and are likely to dismiss talk about the devil and demons as primitive superstition. This was my training as well, but my worldview has changed through my experiences in Thailand. As one mission executive said after hearing my talk about evil spirits, "You have become Thai." Certainly the belief in spirits permeates the culture.

When we began evangelistic visitation in a Lao Song tribal village, we were led to the house of a man very interested in changing his life. We saw that he was very poor. His house was dilapidated with holes in the roof, but he had one huge pig in the back. In the course of our conversation, we asked when he would sell the pig. He said he could not sell it because it was dedicated as an offering for the ancestral spirit feast. He had been a priest at one time, and we asked him if raising that pig to kill, as an offering did not violate the rules of his religion. He replied, "Nothing can free us from the spirits." When he said this it opened my eyes to the importance of spirits in Thai culture.

Theology is often determined by our experience and that of those around us. We are reluctant to accept something that we and our associates do not experience. My theological conclusions are pragmatic. If it is Biblical, is affirmed by church history, works in my life, and in others around me, then I accept it.

We have found that when we face the powers and principalities in the name of Jesus, people are freed. The stories that follow are illustrations of that truth.

RESISTING THE DEVIL

"Submit yourselves, then, to God. Resist the devil, and he will flee from you. Come near to God and he will come near to you." Jas. 4:7-8a

At home in Sam Yaek
(1963-71)

Joan, Ruthanne, Laurie
and David (1965)

The longer we lived in Sam Yaek village, the more we were forced to study the question of the reality of the devil and evil spirits. The villagers had demonic experiences we didn't understand. One night as we were having a nightly devotional at bedtime, Joan and I read the above scripture from James. We discussed whether the concept of the devil was really a name for the abstract principle of evil, or a way to blame somebody else instead of oneself saying, "The devil made me do it." Or, we pondered, is there really an evil personality as described in the Bible? We did not come to a definite conclusion at that time.

The next morning we were getting ready to make the hour's drive from Sam Yaek to speak at the church in Nakhon Pathom. Joan and I usually had tensions when we got ready to go somewhere; I was slow, but Joan was slower. I got ready first and climbed into the Land Rover to wait because we were already late. I knew better than to get into the car to wait, because my patience always ran out quicker while sitting in the car. I got in anyway.

As I waited, I kept telling myself, "Be calm and don't fuss at Joan when she does finally come." But I waited and waited and waited. As soon as she opened the door, I exploded, "You are late again. It is time to be there, and we are just now leaving. You don't have any respect for other people's time." Of course I really meant MY time. Then I brought up how she had spent too much money this month saying, "You always spend too much money." She responded with a few things I had done wrong. It was like putting on a tape that we had recorded long ago. Wherever we started, it kept going from one point of disagreement to another.

As I backed out and drove towards town, I kept getting madder and madder. I became so angry that the thought crossed my mind, "Drive into that tree." Then I remembered the scripture we had discussed the night before. I turned to Joan and said, "Get the devil out of you." As the reader can imagine, she shot back, "You get him out of you first." My furious face probably did look like something was in me.

Then I spoke out loud. "Devil get out, I am drawing near to God." There is no other way to describe the feeling which came over me. It was as if I could feel long talons slowly withdrawing from my heart. Peace flooded in, and Joan saw it in my face. She said the same thing I had said. Then I asked her, "How do you feel?" She replied, "I feel light." Peace settled over the car. Now I was ready to preach the Good news.

I must admit that we still have tensions when we try to leave on time. But we have found that we need to recognize there is an enemy who wants to rob us of our peace, and we had better repent very quickly. If we lose control, then we may be allowing the devil to take over.

WHO ARE YOU SERVING NOW?

"But if serving the Lord seems undesirable to you, then choose for yourselves this day whom you will serve... But as for me and my household, we will serve the Lord."
Josh. 24:15

As missionaries, we know that we should love and serve others. One time I had been out all day trying to show God's love. Joan had also. When I finally came home, I had just about run out of energy to love anyone. I said something to Joan. She was busy and gave a short reply. I was offended and stomped up the stairs.

As I came to the top, my four-year old son, David, crossed in front of me. He did something wrong. I don't remember what it was now, but it must have been something he shouldn't have done. I swatted him as he passed me. He began to cry, but I ignored him and angrily stormed on into the bathroom. As soon as I closed the door, I heard a clear strong voice coming from within asking, "Who are you serving now?"

Mentally I responded, "What is this? Is this some kind of ultimate choice between God and the devil? A father has a right to punish his own son. Besides I did not swat him very hard. He will get over it soon. I'll smile at him, and it will be all right." Once more the voice came, "Who are you serving now?"

We all know it is hard to say, "I'm sorry," even when we know we have done something wrong. It's especially hard if the person is smaller or weaker than we are. I realized I had to make a choice again—"Who am I serving? God, myself or the enemy?"

I had to go back to David to apologize. I don't think I quite used the words, "I'm sorry." The conversation went something like, "David, a few minutes ago I punished you, and it was not your fault. I was angry at your mom." With tears in his eyes, he reached out to me. My tears flowed too, as we hugged each other. We have had clashes since that time, but we have learned to quickly say, "I'm sorry."

David went on to become a major in the US Army Special Forces, but he felt God's call to the mission field. Now, we are working closely together. (See chap. 8, "We Want to Be Free.")

I have learned the truth of the scripture in James 4:10, "Humble yourselves before the Lord, and he will lift you up." -- even in the eyes of your own children.

David explores the
mysteries of the East (1961)

ARE DEMONS REAL? - Crazy with the Spirits

"So he traveled throughout all Galilee, preaching in their synagogues and driving out demons." Mk. 1:39

"His intent was that now, through the church, the manifold wisdom of God should be made known to the rulers and authorities in the heavenly realms, according to his eternal purpose which he accomplished in Christ Jesus our Lord." Eph. 3:10-11

My thinking and understanding of the spirit world was gradually changing when I moved up north from Sam Yaek to Chiang Mai in May of 1971, to teach in the seminary. I remembered that when I was a student in seminary, a professor stated categorically, "Hebrews 13:8 states, 'Jesus Christ is the same yesterday and today and forever.' We do not see evil spirits or demons now, therefore, there were none in Jesus' time. Jesus just used the unscientific language of his day to describe phenomena that we now can explain in purely psychological and biological terms."

My Thai village experiences, however, were causing me to question this. The Thai had as much evidence for their spirits as I did for God, except they did not have a Bible. But the Bible spoke plainly about demons. At first, I did some mental gymnastics. In Thai I would speak like the Bible speaks about Christ delivering people from evil spirits. However, mentally I thought in English, "When they are educated they won't talk like this."

Gradually, as the years passed, it seemed that I questioned more and more my naturalistic teachings which ruled out miracles and spirits. In time, it became clear to me that there was more to this than just semantics.

First, I had seen a paralyzed Lao Song man get up and walk in the name of Jesus (See chap. 6, "You Can Get Up And Walk.") Then, I had another experience of a man whose face changed before my eyes to look like the picture of the medieval devil.

This was followed by the feeling of long talons being withdrawn from my angry heart when I cried, "Devil get out. I am drawing near to God." (See "Resisting the Devil.") The Thai and the Lao Song with whom I had worked had many experiences that made them fear the spirits.

Now I was invited to teach New Testament and Evangelism at the seminary. The question of the reality of evil spirits became crucial in my teaching about how to present the Gospel in Thailand. Since many of the missionaries I worked with were trained like I was, the Thai were reluctant to share their experiences about spirits. They knew westerners would consider them primitive. Now I began to ask Thai leaders to share with me as I was earnestly trying to understand.

Finally, I prayed, "Lord if there really are evil spirits, please let me have some confirming experience. My peers and American church leaders may call me crazy. However, in addition to the testimony of the Bible, church history, and other's experiences, I have my own as well." That very week I had two experiences.

First, a German Marburger missionary, Gerhard Huget, invited me to pray with him for deliverance for a woman at McKean Rehabilitation Center (originally a center for Leprosy treatment), where he served. The Thai said she was "crazy with the spirits." She had expressed a desire to become Christian, and when they prayed with her she began to act oddly, speaking in a strange voice. The Christians had cast out what they believed were several spirits, but every time she went to church for worship or instruction, she immediately fell asleep.

Gerhard, his wife, Charlotte, a Chinese pastor, and I went to her little cottage provided by the hospital for cured patients. At that time people with leprosy were so ostracized that when they came to McKean, they stayed for the rest of their lives. When we prayed, she began to act strangely and then got up, began to dance and speak Chinese.

The Chinese pastor translated for us that the spirit identified itself as a Chinese lord and was declaring, "This woman has come into my house, and I will eat from her. I will get out if you give me a bottle of whisky and twenty baht." Gerhard whispered that she had told him earlier when she was normal she knew no Chinese.

We joined together speaking commands for the Chinese lord to get out in the name of Jesus. We alternated the commands with reading scriptures about Jesus' power over spirits and singing Christian hymns.

Finally, after what seemed to me a very long time, she suddenly collapsed in a heap on the floor. When she got up, she was her normal self. We asked about the Chinese lord, and she told us she had been bothered like this for 17 years. This spirit came into her one night after she had moved into an old house in Bangkok. As I understood, the spirit came in about the same time she had learned she had leprosy.

We told her, "Let's pray to thank God for deliverance." When we began to pray, her voice changed again. This time it was a soft sweet voice of a lady speaking very cultured Thai, completely different from this uneducated village woman's normal language and voice. We asked who she was, and the solicitous voice replied, "I am a witch. I came down to help this

101

poor woman defend herself against mistreatment by that rough lord." She said she came down and got trapped, but now she pleaded very enticingly to be allowed to stay. We found ourselves beginning to feel sorry for the witch, but we cleared our minds and commanded her to leave in the name of Jesus. Suddenly the woman let out a long wail and again fell to the floor. When she sat up she spoke once more in her own voice. We were tired and relieved. After prayer, we left. The pastor promised to return soon.

Later, I heard that the spirit or spirits kept returning. Everyone was so inexperienced. We did not know how we should deal with this. She was more or less left alone.

Whenever anyone prayed with her, the spirits acted up. The church members said she was just acting to get attention. Their reaction was a theological defense. If spirits had been cast out in the power of Jesus then they could not return. It was like I used to tell villagers before I learned better, "Spirits can't bother you after you become a Christian."

I was teaching in the seminary and only made occasional evangelistic visits with my students to the wards of the leprosy hospital. Several times I would meet the woman in the hospital. Each time when I prayed with her she would begin to shake or make strange grunts and sounds until I would command the spirit to stop and get out in the name of Jesus.

Gradually, we learned more from reading others' experiences. I realized that she had been dominated by these spirits so long that she had no defense. The spirits did leave on our command, but would come back again later, and she could not resist their power over her.

A Southern Baptist missionary friend had sent me a tape by Derek Prince about personal deliverance. I went through these steps with the woman as I remembered them from the tape:

1. Honestly confess your own sins.
2. Make the decision to forgive everyone who has hurt you.
3. Examine your past for any involvement with occult powers and renounce them.
4. Declare your faith in Jesus Christ as Lord and Savior.
5. Bind the evil spirits in Jesus' name and then expel them by breathing out.
6. Protect yourself by inviting the Holy Spirit into your life.

I asked her if she could now forgive the Christians who said she was just pretending to get attention. She said, "How can they believe I would deliberately act like this and have others make fun of me? But I will decide to forgive them." She went through the steps, and then I said to her, "Jesus is now in you as Lord. Jesus has given you the authority to forbid the spirits to come back. When you feel their presence, you must tell them you belong to Jesus Christ and to be gone in the name of Jesus."

After that she went back to church, took instruction, was baptized, and then gave a big feast for all her new Christian friends.

About a year later she was married, had a child, and moved away to a village established for those healed of leprosy. I have not seen her for more than 20 years, but every year or so I have asked about her through Christian leaders who know her. They tell me she is still normal and living a Christian life with her family.

This experience gave me hope to deal with cases that we previously left to doctors for medicine or continuous counseling. Of course, not everything is demonic. We do not see demons behind every bush. As Prince urged in his tape, we need to open a file on spirits because we had not considered them real before.

I have given much thought to try and give an answer to my American seminary professor's statement, "If spirits are real, we should experience them around us here." In our American circles most people believe in Jesus Christ. They do not give credence to spirits. Since no one believed in spirits, the spirits could not manifest themselves. If they did, no one dared talk about it for fear of being ridiculed or considered a little "off."

Spiritual powers do work in Christians in unrecognized ways through the sinful and unrepentant areas of their lives, such as hate, prejudice, lust, and greed. As the Christian faith weakens in Western culture, many people are experiencing the reality of spirits and the occult. This is especially true for those using drugs. Today, more and more Western Christians are experiencing the reality of powers and principalities.

A BACK FLIP IN THE LIVING ROOM

"Be quiet!' Jesus said sternly. 'Come out of him!' Then the demon threw the man down before them all and came out without injuring him." Lk. 4:35

"…. Finally Paul became so troubled that he turned around and said to the spirit, 'In the name of Jesus Christ I command you to come out of her!' At that moment the spirit left her." Acts 16:18

A second experience occurred within seven days after I asked God about the reality of evil spirits. It happened at the end of the regular Tuesday night prayer meeting in our home. As we were standing in a circle singing the doxology to close the meeting, a night pick-up taxi drove into our driveway.

The driver was a Thai church elder whom I knew well. He told me, "This man brought his wife to me in the market. He asked me to take them to a priest to drive out the demons that were bothering his wife. I told him, 'The only priest I know who can do that is Jesus.' The man replied, 'Fine! Take me to Jesus.'"

The elder said, "Because it is so late, I didn't know where to take him. I remembered that you had a prayer meeting tonight, so I brought them over here." Then he asked, "May I bring them in?" I said, "Sure, come on in."

As the woman walked into the door, she shrieked and threw up on the floor. Her face was horribly contorted and evil looking. All of us were stunned. We couldn't move. Then an older Overseas Missionary Fellowship (OMF) English missionary, Robin Talbot, who lived with the Hmong tribe and had more experience than I did, whispered to me, "Tell her to shut up in Jesus' name."

On faith, and with more confidence since our earlier experience at McKean, I walked across the room and told her in Thai, "In the name of Jesus, shut up!" The woman fell to the floor in a faint.

I asked her husband what had happened. He explained, "We are part of a traveling medicine team. We show movies to sell medicine. I believe that my wife's former boyfriend cursed her for marrying me. The demons keep bothering her like this." A part of my mind was saying, "What in the world are you doing?" But I spoke out in faith and told her husband, "Jesus will deliver her if you let him. Will you give me permission to remove the charms and pray with her?"

He agreed. I began by removing a double handful of charms from her wrists and neck. Then I bent over her and was just about to command the spirits to release her. She suddenly arose and turned a back flip from a squatting position in front of our couch.

She glared at me as we crouched face to face. Her eyes had no focus, but were animal-like with a powerful force of hate pouring out. I regained control of myself and said, "I am an ambassador of Jesus Christ. I come in his name. I command you evil spirit to come out in the name of Jesus Christ and never return."

Focus came back to her eyes. She looked around, noticed that she had her nightclothes on and asked, "Where am I? Can you come out like this?" Her husband gave her his jacket to cover up.

There were four senior medical students at the meeting that night. They were new believers, so they gave her short words of testimony and encouragement. Then I asked her, "Would you like to accept Jesus as Lord and Savior?" She nodded "yes," and I led her in a prayer of confession and acceptance.

By now we were all exhausted. We closed the meeting with one verse of "Amazing Grace." The woman joined in and sang with us. Her beautiful face radiated purity and joy. A half-hour earlier she was a horrible looking witch.

We had medical expertise present for validation and evaluation of the event. Dr. Trevor Smith, an Australian missionary doctor heading medical work at McKean Rehabilitation Center, was there along with the four senior medical students.

The next night we asked the Thai elder, who had brought the afflicted woman, to go ask her family if we could visit them at the place where they were staying. We wanted to go and pray with the young woman who had been delivered. He came back with this report:

> As I walked in, the woman was shaking and possessed with another spirit. She shouted at me in a man's voice, 'That spirit last night was only a little one. I am the Prince and NO ONE gets rid of me!' Then her husband told me that they did not want us to come. They are too afraid. I have to admit I could feel that evil power trying to get me too.

Since they would not give permission, we felt we did not have the right to go, and they moved on. Even though we were disappointed that we could not follow up on the young woman, that experience was confirmation for me in answer to my prayer request for validation.

I have had many other experiences with spirits since then. I do not fully understand, but it is as the Bible says: evil spirits are REAL personalities, which can impose themselves on humans.

This is not just semantics for a type of human mental illness. Certainly, mental illness is real. However, it should be recognized that some illnesses can be treated by deliverance.

These experiences demonstrate the reality of the power of Christ. We do not have to be afraid. "The reason the Son of God appeared was to destroy the devil's work." (1 Jn. 3:8)

TWO PSYCHOLOGY PROFESSORS

"So do not fear, for I am with you; do not be dismayed, for I am your God. I will strengthen you and help you..."
Is. 41:10

"The Lord will rescue me from every evil attack and bring me safely to his heavenly kingdom. To him be glory for ever and ever. Amen." II Tim. 4:18

"Cast all your anxiety on him because he cares for you."
1 Pet. 5:7

Professor Nantiga Yamsrual is board chairperson of the Bamrungtam Church in Nakhon Pathom, and is an associate professor of psychology at Silapakon University. She told me the following story and has written it to distribute in Thai:

> I grew up in a Christian family in Chiang Mai, attended Dara (Christian school) and was a member of First Church. In spite of the Christian upbringing, I had three major doubts: 1. Is Jesus God? 2. Are there really angels? 3. What is the importance of the Bible? I had a firm belief in God and prayed to him. I tried to be a good person, but I didn't really study God's word.
>
> After receiving my master's degree in psychology, I became a professor in the university. I seldom went to church because I was satisfied to spend my time enjoying my work, my family, and my friends.
>
> About 28 years ago I became ill with terrible bouts of asthma and other allergies. High blood pressure developed, followed by bruises all over my body and severe aching in my hips and legs. It was very difficult to walk. I didn't pray much to God, even though my mother

told me to do so. I went to a friend who used ancient herbal methods and massage, which helped me feel better.

July 6, 1990, was a very important day for me. My close friend invited me to go with her to meet someone who might help heal me, but she didn't give me the details. I went out of curiosity. However, to my surprise when I walked in the door, a medium in a full trance spoke with a spirit's voice directly to me.

It identified itself as the guardian spirit ruler of the provincial cornerstone. It said, "Child, I cannot heal you. You are the child of God. I can't help you unless Jesus gives permission because he is looking after you."

Then the spirit ruler spoke to my friend saying, "Jesus Christ is God, and his blood helps people. I cannot help her because she is the child of God and is a Christian. There is a bright red cross on her chest. She has two sacred Bibles on her bookshelf and a picture of Jesus in her bedroom."

Later another spirit, identifying itself as the ruler of the dead, said to me, "When you die, an angel will come to get you." I asked about the place the angel would take me. The spirit replied, "I don't know. You go up there to be with Jesus. I am not allowed. I come to get the others."

I was stunned, and I was humbled to realize that even in my half belief, Jesus was taking care of me. When I came in the room, I still had doubts. I had thought that if Jesus Christ was God, why didn't he heal me.

After this encounter, there were no more doubts. I was certain of four things: 1. Jesus is God. Whether he heals me or not, he is still God; 2. I knew the Bible was sacred, and I was excited to read the good news of Jesus Christ; 3. I knew that angels were real; 4. I had a better understanding of the deep mystery that God is really with everyone who believes, just as the writers of the Bible have recorded. Since that time I have fully dedicated myself to the service of Jesus Christ.

Prof. Nantiga

Bamrungtam Church
Nakhon Pathom

Professor Tussaneeya Wongchant has a master's degree in psychology, and is the head of the psychology department at Payap University. Once, while I was acting chaplain at the university, she sat beside me as I drove the teachers to a faculty retreat. At the top of the mountain pass north of Chiang Mai, we saw many spirit houses put up as offerings to the "Lord of the Pass."

I commented to the teacher that it was interesting to see that the Thai believe in many levels of spirits, from the local spirits of the land, to rulers of the mountain passes, and the spirit lord of Thailand. It seemed that it should be easy for the Thai to accept a supreme spirit – the Holy Spirit of God. There are many authority levels in Thailand, from the farmer, to the village headman, to the governor, and finally to the Palace. It seems logical that there would be a Spirit above all spirits. She seemed interested.

On these retreats I always prayed that God would lead me to someone who would be open to believe in Jesus. I prayed about talking with Tussaneeya, but there never seemed to be an opportunity.

Finally, the morning before we were to leave, I called her aside. Later, she said she really wondered, "Why would the chaplain want to talk to me?" I went through the Campus Crusade's "Four Spiritual Laws" booklet on why we need Jesus. I asked her if she would like to pray to ask Jesus to come into her heart and be her Lord and Savior. She nodded "yes."

I showed her the sample prayer and told her it was not a magic formula, but a guide to open her heart and invite Jesus in. She prayed with me, and then it was time to go into the next meeting.

Later, she told me that two other Christian teachers had shared their faith and encouraged her that afternoon. She amazed me with the rest of her story. She said,

> When I was 16 years old, a spirit appeared to me and said, "I am a wandering spirit with no place to live. Let me live with you." I strongly objected, but the spirit came back again and again, trying to take control of my life. I have done everything to resist it, including the study of psychology and collecting many charms to ward off that evil power.

I always carry with me a magic cloth as protection. The night after we prayed, I looked at that cloth and realized I didn't need it anymore. Jesus had answered my prayer and was protecting me. The power of Jesus is stronger than that of the spirits.

About two weeks later I stopped by her apartment and picked her up, along with others, to go to a week of spiritual renewal at the university. As she opened the door she handed me a large plastic sack and said, "These are all the talismans, charms and images I have had in my room. I don't need them anymore."

Her younger sister, Vanlapa, teaches financial management at the university. The sisters shared the apartment. When Vanlapa came home and found all of their sacred emblems removed, she was very angry and afraid.

Her sister persuaded her to go to the renewal meetings on the basis that they would pray to Jesus to help their mother get well. At the meeting, the younger sister prayed to receive Jesus so they could join together and pray for their mother's healing. Those prayers were answered, and the mother was healed.

They have had many other experiences with God. Eight of their 10 brothers and sisters, as well as a number of nieces and nephews, have now received Christ. At present, Tussaneeya is vice chairman of the board at Payap University Church, and her sister is treasurer.

Prof. Tussaneeya's baptism with
Chaplain Somboon Tassalee and Allan

Payap University Chapel

A SNAKE AROUND MY ARMS

"Now the serpent was more crafty than any of the wild animals the Lord God had made." Gen.3:1

"For God knows that when you eat of it your eyes will be opened, and you will be like God, knowing good and evil." Gen. 3:5

"...that ancient serpent called the devil or Satan, who leads the whole world astray. He was hurled to the earth, and his angels with him." Rev. 12:9

Lek, one of our actresses at the Christian Communications Institute(CCI), came into our building one day very excited. She said, "I want to tell you about a very good dramatist, Sujinda Chaiyagunsarakron. He graduated last year from Chiang Mai University and has spent a year as assistant director making a movie. I spoke with him, and he is interested in what we, at CCI, are doing. Let me bring him to meet you." I agreed, and we set up an appointment.

That was in 1983. The communists were beginning to give up in the mountains around the borders of Thailand. In talking with Sujinda, I learned that he, like many university students, was very idealistic and committed to helping the poor. He said that he had not been an "official communist," but he had believed, as they did, that only a revolution could change society. He was convinced that without the force of a gun, the rich people would never share with the poor.

He had used drama while he was in the university to recruit revolutionaries to join the communists in the mountains. Now he had become disillusioned with the communists and realized that they could never live up to their ideals. Certainly they could not bring about democracy.

I told him we were trying to change society with love, specifically through the love of Jesus Christ. He replied that he had no religious beliefs, but if I would take him that way he would be willing to study our religion. I accepted him on that basis. We had learned to trust God to call people to faith or let them move on. There were very few Christians in the dramatic arts.

Sujinda as one of the Chiang Mai martyrs
in the historical drama which he produced

His genius in dramatic production was obvious from the beginning. After about eight months he surprised me by asking for baptism. Following a period of instruction, we went up to a little stream on the mountain for the baptism.

At Easter, six months later, Joan was directing the first production of "Beyond Death." It was a modern musical drama of the life of Christ written by Sunshine who was introduced in chapter 1, "Make Me Fall in Love." Sujinda was in charge of lighting. The play was given at the First Church, Chiang Mai. It was presented in three parts, with one part given each of the last three nights during Holy Week.

As the production developed, I sensed that Sujinda was having trouble. I invited him to our home one night and asked him directly about my impressions. He admitted, "Yes, I have a problem. When I was baptized I didn't really believe in Jesus. I just went through the training and the ceremony to see if anything would happen. It didn't."

Challenging him, I suggested that he pray again and sincerely ask Jesus to come into his heart one more time. He agreed, so I led him in a prayer, confessing sin, and inviting Jesus to be his Lord and Savior. As he finished the prayer, he shook, held his arms together in front of his face and whispered, "It's like a snake wrapped around my arms!"

Immediately, I cast that snake out in the name of Jesus. He gave a sigh and relaxed his arms saying, "It's gone." After more prayer and encouragement, he returned to the drama and did an excellent job.

He worked with us about 10 years and then moved on. He has become prominent in television production, especially in costume design. He comes back once a year to help CCI polish up one of its major productions.

In addition to his legacy of excellent Christian drama productions, he left us some "doodles." One day while we were rehearsing a folk drama, I watched him scribbling with his pen. When I looked closer, I was impressed. He had produced a drawing of deep theological meaning in ancient Thai style.

On the following pages are three of his best drawings with explanations. I gave each drawing a scriptural title after he gave me its meaning. Note the prominence of the snake.

ADAM AND EVE

Adam covers his face in shame and points to Eve to indicate that she caused the trouble by taking the fruit. With her left hand, Eve refuses to accept the blame, and points an accusing finger toward the snake holding the forbidden fruit. Sujinda has given the snake a giant's head because, in Thai culture, everyone accepts that the giant from Indian mythology is evil. The large snake is often found on either side of the steps going into Buddhist temples, and is considered to be an emblem of good protection.

Little serpent heads come out from the back of the giant, adding to the sense of evil, and the wings show Satan's great mobility. The snake curls around Adam and Eve to indicate they are within its power. Curling up like a wisp of smoke from the bottom center of the picture is an ancient Thai design representing the Holy Spirit of God, confronting Adam, Eve and the snake.

"…the woman you gave me …" Gen. 3:12

NOAH

In the foreground are four carousing figures. Two are holding elaborate chalices from which fumes rise like snakes – through their hair and around their bodies – to indicate the deadly potency of the drink. Another is smoking an opium pipe with the smoke rising to end with the open mouth of the serpent at the man's neck. They do not realize that they are in the coils of Satan, who holds up his hand, indicating that all are under his spell. The two figures to the right represent evangelists trying to communicate salvation before it is too late. One holds a heart-shaped mirror so the worldly crowd might see that they are made in the image of God. The other evangelist points heavenward.

Inside the ark, representing the church, is the New World. It is decorated with hearts to show that the new creation is filled with love. Underneath, and lifting up the ark, is the vaporous, faintly seen representation of the Holy Spirit of God, saving the world through the church.

"… as in the days of Noah …" Mt. 24:37

THE TOWER OF BABEL

This drawing is a Thai interpretation of the Tower of Babel story. It shows the different levels held up by kneeling, crying, suffering, chained humanity. At the top, the "thumbs up" is a Thai expression to say, "We are the best." They don't realize that their brain is held in the hands of Satan, whose snake-like body entwines the whole structure. The evil giant head is staring at the thin trail of vapor representing the inescapable presence of God.

At the bottom of the picture a woman looks, with a tear in her eye, at the broken image of God in the heart-shaped mirror. The trail of vapor connects the broken image with the confrontation of Satan at the top. A man kneeling on the structure throws up his arm in fear as he turns with Satan to face God.

"…let us make a name for ourselves …" Gen. 11:4

MOSES AND THE VOICES

"What is all this that you are doing for the people? Why are you doing this all alone…." Exodus 18:14

In March, 1991, Sujinda gave Allan this picture as a helpful reminder in administrating the Christian Communications Institute.

CONFESSING AND FORGIVING

"For if you forgive men when they sin against you, your heavenly Father will also forgive you. But if you do not forgive men their sins, your Father will not forgive your sins." Mt. 6:14-15

In confronting evil, both within and without, the necessity for forgiving others cannot be underestimated. The Thai word for unforgiving means "to carry the punishment." This is a clear demonstration of the truth that when we punish other people in our hearts and minds because of what they have done to us, we are really carrying the punishment inside of ourselves. Refusing to forgive also prevents our overcoming evil. Two examples follow:

WHAT A SWEET TUNE

About 20 years ago, our CCI Evangelism Team was in Petchaburi Province, holding a week of evangelism and renewal in the Christian school.

Student assembly, Arun Pradit School in Petchaburi

125

Toward the end of the week, a Christian teacher asked us to go to his home, because his wife was ready to be freed from the spirits. She was a medium with a whole room set aside for the worship of spirits and gods.

I went through the steps of leading her to Christ and renouncing of the spirits. When I commanded, in Jesus' name, that the spirits come out, her face and voice changed, becoming much more masculine. The spirit laughed and mocked.

After commanding for some time, we began to sing a very vigorous chorus, celebrating the victory of Jesus over the devil and his angels. The spirit in the medium looked at us, sneered, scoffed, and laughed, saying over and over again, "What a sweet tune."

Praying silently, I asked God why we could not cast out the spirit. It came to me that I was angry with one of our performers. I told her to be quiet behind the curtain because people could hear.

Who can stay angry with such pretty girls?

. Then I went out to the front and still heard her talking. I had stalked back again and strongly rebuked her. I felt she had not shown me the proper respect.

Now, facing this evil spirit, I realized the anger was still in my heart. I had overreacted, because the actress had disobeyed me and hurt my pride. I prayed to be forgiven and, also, forgave her.

Then, I turned to the spirit with much more confidence. This time when I commanded in Jesus' name, the woman's face and voice returned to normal. The spirit had gone. I didn't see it, but her husband said he saw green fire coming out of my fingers. We cleaned out her spirit room and dedicated it to Jesus.

There had to be confession and forgiveness to clear the way for the power of God to flow through us. I was like a clogged water pipe that had to be cleaned out before the water could flow.

WE HAVEN'T SPOKEN FOR ALMOST A YEAR

The second experience occurred that night when we called for people to come forward for decision and prayer. Many came forward. There was one woman who asked prayer for her troubled heart. When we started to pray, she began to wail loudly in an unnatural way. When she wouldn't stop, we commanded the spirits to be gone. She still disturbed everyone with her moaning and groaning.

We took her outside and she quieted down, but every time we started to pray with her she began the loud wailing again. Finally, we took her to her home. When we asked whether there was anyone she had not forgiven, she said, "Yes! my sister-in-law who lives in the same house. We have not spoken to each other for almost a year."

After talking with the sister-in-law and the woman, they both agreed to forgive each other. Then we cast out the spirit. She became normal and there was no more wailing.

As I have already mentioned, this happened 20 years ago. Recently the CCI troupe returned from another week of evangelism at the same Petchaburi school. One of the new performers in the troupe said a woman came to her in Petchaburi and said, "When I was a little girl, Achan Eubank cast a spirit out of my mother." The woman asked to send greetings to me, and asked if I still remembered the night. It is still vivid in my mind.

The pictures above are from a very popular Thai Folk Drama (Likay) based on our experiences with the spirits in Petchaburi

BITTER ROOTS

"See to it that no one misses the grace of God and that no bitter root grows up to cause trouble and defile many." Heb. 12:15

"I tell you the truth, whatever you bind on earth will be bound in heaven, and whatever you loose on earth will be loosed in heaven." Mt. 18:18

I think our generation tried its best to base education on complete confidence in reason. Everything had to have a rational explanation. The next generation turned to drugs because they knew reason didn't satisfy, and they wanted experience. In our day, we called it "being a modern man," and were taught to "adapt our theology to fit the modern man." That, of course, is very dated because now we must include the word "woman."

We really were not so modern. I believe we were closer to the Sadducees. The Sadducees were the "modern men of their generation," having little "truck" with the supernatural. Acts 23:8 states, "The Sadducees say there is no resurrection, and that there are neither angels nor spirits, but the Pharisees acknowledge them all." We were taught to believe that reason would solve everything, and psychology could be a pure science. Many Christian teachers had room for God but nothing else supernatural.

After ten years in Thailand, we were opening up to the reality of the supernatural. I have saved this story until the end of this chapter because it is probably the most controversial.

In my forties, I suddenly realized that I was having unhealthy thoughts about sex. I had read in the pastoral care books that this often happened to men at about this time in their lives. In Thailand, this is the age when men take second wives.

In the earlier story, "Are Demons Real?" I referred to a tape by Derek Prince sent by a missionary friend. Prince recommended that we check out the presence of spirits, who might be controlling areas of our lives, even though we are Christians. Prince said, just as there are areas of the city where the mayor is not in control, there may be areas of our lives which are weak and not surrendered to Christ's control. This may allow spirits to get talons into us. I had earlier announced to villagers that if they became Christians, then spirits couldn't bother them. Now, I found I had to "eat" those words.

Out of respect for my Baptist's friend's recommendation, I decided to try the steps of deliverance outlined in the tape:

1. Confessed again every sin I could think of.
2. Forgave everyone I could think of.
3. Renounced any dabbling in the occult. (I couldn't think of anything.)
4. Invited Jesus again to be my Lord and Savior.
5. Commanded any evil thing to come out in the name of Jesus. This is the authority given to us in Mt. 18:18 and other scriptures. Especially, I commanded, "You demon of sexual thoughts – get out of my life in Jesus' name." Then I began to breathe out and expel any evil thing in me without speaking. I didn't feel anything strange happen. On later reflection, I don't believe that there were spirits involved. Any bad thoughts were dealt with through confession. (Of course, the war between flesh and spirit is not over with one battle.)
6. Protected myself by asking the Holy Spirit to come in and fill my life again.

A few nights later, I woke up in the middle of the night with the clear thought, "Cast out a spirit of bitterness against your mother." I recalled the psychological tests that I took in applying for the mission field. The tests indicated a possible problem in the relationship with my mother, but not enough to affect my work. I would not have described my feelings as bitterness, but I realized I had a fear of being dominated, even though she poured out all her love and encouragement on me. Some might say she spoiled her only son.

I asked Joan to get up and go with me to the bathroom and close the door so the children wouldn't be disturbed by any noise. I sat down and quickly went through the first four steps again. Then, I cast out the spirit of bitterness. I began to feel a rumble rise deep inside of me. It was as if my mind was detached, observing what was going on. A roar of anger came up my throat and out of my mouth. I saw Joan's face, white and wide-eyed, watching, as I felt my face contort with anger. Then it was gone, and I felt peace. I prayed again for the in-filling of the Holy Spirit and for protection and guidance.

There was an immediate change in how I felt about my mother. I could find no resentment in myself, only love and appreciation. I also felt an understanding of her alienation from her immigrant European father because he did not support her desire to finish college.

One of my greatest sins of neglect is in letter writing. I only wrote my parents three or four times a year, but for the next six months I wrote every week. Then I gradually slipped back into old habits. I still feel shame and regret at this failure to express my love, respect, and gratitude for my parents more regularly.

From that day on, there was a qualitative difference in my relationship with my mother. I wanted to go see her at every opportunity. We enjoyed our times together whenever I was home. As her health began to slip, she expressed some doubts about future life. She allowed me to read Jesus' comforting promises and lead her again in a confirming prayer to accept Jesus Christ as her Lord and Savior.

Perhaps she had been afflicted (not possessed) by the demonic in the alienation from her family, and it was coming down through the generations to me. If I had not dealt with it, this demonic influence might have gone on down to my children.

I shared this experience in the prayer meeting with our fellow missionaries. Our children were there and heard it. We felt they needed to know about these things. During this same period people were bringing Thai students to our home during the prayer meetings, and we would cast out spirits in the kitchen while everyone else prayed for us in the living room. Our daughter's bedroom was above the kitchen. They still tell about hearing the spirit's voices as they left. Joan and another lady came and prayed with Ruthanne and Laurie for protection. Later when they went to high school in Bangkok, these experiences enabled them to cast out a spirit from their classmate.

Allan and Joan with children: Ruthanne, David, Suewannee, and Laurie in Chiang Mai. (1975)

About a week after I had cast out the spirit of bitterness, our 12-year old son, David, came to me and asked, "How did you get rid of that spirit?" I told him the six steps and we went through them. I don't remember what he confessed, but it wasn't very much.

Then I had him take authority and cast out any evil spirit which might be inside of him. After he cast out the spirits, I told him to exhale in deep breaths and let go of whatever would come out. As he breathed out I prayed, casting out spirits in the name of Jesus.

The thought came to my mind, "a spirit of fear." He had not mentioned fear, but I cast it out in Jesus name. His stomach constricted and a long wail rose up in his chest and came out of his mouth.

After the noise was gone, David said, "What was that?" and I said, "Was that you?" In a hushed tone he replied, "I don't think so." I remembered his fear. His job had been to close the gate about 50 yards in front of our house every night. He tried to act brave, but I felt there was fear when he went out. One night I sent him about 300 yards to the seminary dormitory to call someone. He came back in a cold sweat and whispered with fear, "It was dark, and there was no one there."

I asked David when he had first begun to feel fear regularly. He said it began one night while the family was in the States on furlough. He was in the fourth grade at that time. Joan and I had gone to speak. There was another lady in the house, but he was in a room alone, watching a horror movie on TV. It causes me to wonder how much these horror movies are affecting our children.

Since we cast out that spirit, David says he still feels afraid in dangerous situations, but he actually seeks out and

133

enjoys such situations. He joined the U.S. Army Rangers and then became a major in the Special Forces. His last job was commanding a freefall HALO (High Altitude Low Opening.) unit. He and his men bailed out of an airplane at 20,000 to 30,000 ft. in the dark, watching their altimeters until they reached 3,000 ft., and then opened their chutes together to glide in under the radar. He has climbed Mt. McKinley in Alaska and run before the bulls in Spain. As a missionary, he trains and leads units with medicine, food, Bibles, and encouragement to help internally displaced people in very dangerous areas.

David, Karen, Sahale - 2 ½, Suuzanne – 6 months

Many may find the idea of casting spirits out of oneself difficult to accept. It is possible that I worked a psychological trick on myself, but I do not believe it. Casting out evil spirits is Bible based, and I have seen it work in others. I have tried it, and it changed an area of my life and my son's life for the better. Therefore, so far as I am concerned, I have tested it, and I recommend that others try these steps of deliverance. When we go to a doctor, often he isn't exactly sure what the problem may be. He gives us a prescription to try and says, "Come back next week, or call me." Deliverance is another way to check and see if the symptoms are relieved. The problem may be psychological, medical, spiritual, or a combination.

CHAPTER 5

SAVE US FROM DEATH

"Since the children have flesh and blood, he too shared in their humanity so that by his death he might destroy him who holds the power of death – that is, the devil – and free those who all their lives were held in slavery by their fear of death." Heb. 2:14-15

IT'S ALL RIGHT - Korea

"For God so loved the world that he gave his one and only Son, that whoever believes in him shall not perish but have eternal life." Jn. 3:16

    In traveling around the world, I have often asked people, "What was the first verse you recall memorizing when you were a child?" John 3:16 was most often mentioned. It was the first scripture I remember as well. This excellent summary of the hope we have in Jesus reassures children that they need not be afraid of death. No matter what happens, we are all in the security of God's loving care. Scriptural promises learned in childhood remain with us as adults and lead us to turn to God in every crisis, even unto death.

    The Korean War was going on in June, 1951, when I graduated from Texas A&M with a degree in geological engineering and a regular Army 2nd lt. Commission in the Corps of Engineers. After basic officer's training at Ft. Belvoir,

Virginia, the Army sent me to Korea in charge of a platoon of combat engineers. The first night when I reached my unit, I had a small but memorable experience of God's reassurance.

My platoon was assigned to build a Bailey bridge across the Han Tan River. (The Bailey is like a large steel erector set.) The Chinese had invaded North Korea and had pushed the UN troops back down along the 38th parallel. We were building the bridge over the Han Tan in a blackout to keep from drawing Chinese artillery fire.

It was pitch black. We could barely see the other side of the river. We didn't know what was over there. I felt it was my responsibility to take a small patrol and scout out the other bank to make sure there was no enemy. We put the small boat ashore and fanned out to walk up the bank. I began to feel the awful fear of what might happen.

We were young, strong, trained and well armed, but I began to fear that my own men would bring down fire because of the noise their boots were making as we walked on the loose gravel along the bank. Even though we could not see each other in the dark, I was afraid that the enemy would see or hear us. I prayed quietly, "Lord help me." Now on reflection, I wish I had prayed for my men in that moment, but actually the prayer was a purely selfish, "Lord help me." Immediately there was the soft reassuring answer, "It's all right."

We completed the patrol and returned to our bridge construction. The next morning when we could see, I laughed at my fears. The enemy must have been miles away all the time, but that still small voice of quiet reassurance never left me. Because of this experience, I opened my Bible each night after crawling into my sleeping bag and read a few verses by flashlight before I fell asleep. I went through the war without injury.

I had a part in putting four bridges across this river. The night in the story, we were replacing a bridge knocked out by a Chinese bridge floating down river in a flood. The river rose 20 to 40 ft. during the July and August rains, and we had to build low to keep out of enemy fire. I was standing on that same river bank site supervising construction of the fourth bridge, this time a pontoon bridge, when orders came to send me home.

Remains of a 490 ft. Bailey Bridge our unit put across the Han Tan River near Chorwan, Korea. (August, 1952)

The reality of that inner voice, "It is all right." did not necessarily mean that I would not be killed. However, the assurance which it gave has remained with me as a missionary in the deep jungle on elephant expeditions; with the drama troupe in communist guerrilla controlled areas; and in bandit villages. Often, I visited areas in rural Thailand, where no one ever went outside at night without a gun or, at least, a long knife. Villagers would ask me, "Why do you go out unarmed?" I always told them, "God won't let me die until my work for him is done, and even then, whatever happens, it's all right because God is with me."

Officers of A Co., 11th Engr. Combat Bn. (1953)
Front: Duane Ungs, Joe Clem Back: Jim Tolley,
Allan Eubank, Sylvester Gilbertson, Devereaux Cannon
These were the company officers when Joan came to sing

Blasting a road through the mountains for defense
on the 38th Parallel

A REAL CHRISTIAN FUNERAL

"Where, O death, is your victory? Where, O death, is your sting?" I Cor. 15:55

As our minds began to open up to the reality of the supernatural, Rob Collins, a longtime Presbyterian missionary friend and colleague at the seminary, and I began to discuss the reality of spirits. The chaplain in McCormick Hospital (Christian) told us a young Christian mother, Kanchana, had come from Chiang Rai Province, north of Chiang Mai. People said she was afflicted by evil spirits. Rob and I went to see her doctor and found that she had a kind of congenital anemia. The doctor said that people with this kind of disease generally died in their thirties.

When we went to see the lady, we asked her about the spirits. She admitted that even though they were Christians, in their frustration, they had consulted a spirit doctor. We asked her to confess this sin to God and ask forgiveness, which she did. Then we used an exorcism prayer that was in the Anglican Prayer Book, and we prayed for her healing. We saw no visible signs, but she seemed relieved and was glad that we had prayed.

Later, we received word from the village that at about the same time we had prayed, the spirit doctor cried out with the voice of the spirit, "It's too hot. I can't stay with her any longer." The patient recovered her strength and returned to her village. Rob and I celebrated and thanked God for the recovery.

About a month later, the woman came back, sick again. This time there was no mention of the spirits when we spoke with her, so we prayed and anointed her with oil. She regained her strength and went home. Again we rejoiced and thanked God.

Another month or two later, she returned for the third time. We prayed and prayed, and had our prayer group pray. Many others also prayed. She returned to her home so very weak we felt it unlikely we would ever see her again, even after all the prayer.

Several months later, I received word that she had died, and I felt very depressed. We had prayed and prayed, praised and praised, cast out the spirits, anointed with oil and still she died. Shortly thereafter, I was told that her husband was out in my front yard and wanted to see me. I did not want to go out, but I knew I had to face him. I expected him to rebuke me or show his anger toward God for not answering our prayers.

His warm smile and his outpouring of enthusiasm surprised me. He told me that before his wife died the Holy Spirit spoke through her, and she became an oracle, giving everyone a word of truth about himself or herself. She called the church elders. When they came, she pointed out their sins. They accepted her criticism and repented. Revival broke out in the village, and he wanted Rob and me to know.

Later, I received a letter dated July 20, 1972, from Frank Younkin, a Presbyterian agricultural missionary friend in that area. He wrote:

Knowing your interest in Nang Kanchana, I thought you might be interested in a resume of her last days. She died physically last Sunday at 7:00 A.M. with an expression on her face of complete peace. Three weeks prior to that she had gone into a coma for two hours. As she came out of that state, she told the people assembled that she had been with Jesus.... She then expressed a very deep concern for the church in that area. She said the revival was like receiving a bowl of hot curry that had now grown cold. More of the church members needed to truly repent and give themselves to Christ. She also chided all those present who had been crying. When she finally went to be with Christ, there would be no more problems.

She led the group in singing, keeping perfect time. Then she called several people to her. When she touched them, she would tell them all the things that they had not yet confessed and warned that time was short. Christ would soon come again – they must confess…. Thus for the past three weeks, her household has had a continual succession of people coming to listen to Kanchana's witness. They have kept count of how many people she has led to Christ. When she did definitely die, there were no tears, but rather a feeling that she had truly passed into the better life. This feeling of joy continued right up to the grave. This, for me, was the truly Christian attitude.

A few years later, I took the Likay Troupe up north to her village. The people were still talking about the wonderful things, which happened through her death. Her daughter, who was only a baby then, now has her master's degree and works at Payap University. All the prayers that we invested were not in vain, just as the Lord has promised.

A FAITHFUL WITNESS

"Fight the good fight of the faith. Take hold of the eternal life to which you were called when you made your good confession in the presence of many witnesses." 1 Tim. 6:12

"I have fought the good fight, I have finished the race, I have kept the faith." 2 Tim. 4:7

When we first moved to Chiang Mai in 1971, we started a prayer meeting in our home. One Tuesday evening in 1974, Dr. Ed McDaniel, the missionary doctor who pioneered birth control in Thailand, came to our prayer gathering. He asked us to pray for his wife, Charlotte, saying she had just been diagnosed with terminal cancer.

He said, "I am hesitant to ask prayer for healing because there is practically no hope. She has about six more months. I want you to pray for strength, for as little pain as possible, and for the ability to be good witnesses for Jesus Christ as her health declines."

We gathered and held hands in a circle. As we asked the Lord how to pray, we felt led to speak out,

Doctor, If you believe it is God's will that your wife die of cancer, why are you fighting this disease? You have just sent to the U.S. to get the best medicine you can find to fight the cancer. You know that if you could find a way to eradicate this terrible evil from the world, you would do it. We don't understand all that is behind this, but if you can fight cancer with all your might, why can't we, your friends, join you in the battle the way Jesus has told us to, by praying?

Then we began to pray for healing. Charlotte

made rapid recovery. In a few months she was up. She flew home for her daughter's wedding, and returned full of renewed energy and testimony. It was a time of rejoicing for all of us.

After about a year, however, her health began to deteriorate again. This time Dr. Ed called many elders to come and anoint her with oil, according to James 5:14-15. We prayed and prayed, but her condition continued to decline.

Finally, one morning Dr. John Guyer, the Missionary Head Doctor of McCormick Hospital, called to say Charlotte's time was near. I went immediately and found her alone in the room, as Dr. Ed had gone to the airport. Her eyes were open for a moment. Then she slipped into a coma with no sign of awareness.

I began to read the scriptures to her even though she was in the coma, because I remembered my own experience about 25 years earlier. I had extremely high malaria fever (106.9 F.), and went into a coma. My two doctor friends were beside the bed discussing the best way to help me. Suddenly, their words burned into my memory when one whispered, "Now, let's not tell anyone that we did not agree on the treatment." They must have come to the right decision, because I am still here

Later, I heard about the testimony of the Captain of the ship "Logos" when the ship visited Thailand. He said he was led to pray to receive Jesus Christ by a nurse who was talking to him while he was in a coma after a heart attack. No one ever expected that he could take charge of a ship again, but here he was - in great health.

I began to read out loud some of those wonderful encouraging scriptures, promising God's eternal presence, care, and love. Dr. Ed and a nurse came in as I read. He motioned for me to continue. Then a group of Charlotte's nursing students came into the room and asked to sing. As they sang some hymns, the doctor turned on his tape recorder to record their lovely voices. I noticed a movement of the nurse, and I turned to see the nurse closing Charlotte's eyes. She had gone. Dr. Ed was still watching and recording the nursing students. When their hymn finished, he turned and saw that his wife had died. He paused for just a moment. Then he took her hand and turned to the students to say,

> My wife asked me to speak for her when this time came. She wants to reassure you. 'It's all right. I am with God. Jesus has prepared a place for me and has come to take me home. God is taking care of my family. But there will come a day when each of you will be as I am now. If you are not ready for that day, then we want to invite you to allow Jesus to come into your heart to give you the comfort, peace and assurance that I have.'

When Dr. Ed finished, he asked me to pray. I was so choked up I could hardly speak. Charlotte had carefully written out how she wanted her funeral service conducted. In those days black and white were "musts" in Thai culture, but she asked that everyone wear colorful dress to make her funeral a time of celebration. And it was.

I believe prayer had a part in giving our friend more time to attend her daughter's wedding. It also gave her time to make arrangements for her family and to prepare her final testimony. That gift of time made an impact on many lives. She had indeed been a faithful witness. The word of her testimony is still bearing fruit today.

There are three generations of McDaniels who have served as missionary doctors in Thailand. Dr. Ed's father served in the south, Dr. Ed in the north, and his son, Dr. Phil, served for more than 20 years in the Kwai River Christian Hospital, Sangkhlaburi.

Dr. Ed and Charlotte McDaniel

We do not understand God's will concerning disease, but that experience taught us that we are not to give up. If we ask, the Holy Spirit will teach us how to pray. Then we must pray without ceasing, just as the doctors keep on giving medicine.

A missionary prayer group representing six denominations at the McDaniels' after a service for Charlottte - laying on hands and anointing with oil. (June, 1976)

Front left to right, Joan Eubank, Heather Smith, Rosemary Chartres, Charlotte McDaniel, Georgina Stott, Samai Panchaipum, Herb Grether, Back Row - left, Allan Eubank, Trevor Smith, Paul Manikam, Gordon Byers, Eugene Morse, C. W. Callaway, Lois Callaway, Bill Chartres. Photo by Dr. Ed.

THE DEATH OF A GRANDSON

"In this world you will have trouble. But take heart! I have overcome the world." Jn. 16:33b

"During the days of Jesus' life on earth, he offered up prayers and petitions with loud cries and tears to the one who could save him from death, and he was heard because of his reverent submission. Although he was a son, he learned obedience from what he suffered..." Heb. 5:7-8

For most of my ministry, I had dealt with the problem of suffering and death more from a faith and theory position, rather than from practical experience. We had few troubles of our own, and my experience was in helping others deal with their trouble. But then real suffering came home to my family.

My daughter, Ruthanne, the second of our four children, had married a fine young Thai man nicknamed "Oot." They built a lovely Thai style teak house next door to ours in Chiang Mai. Ruthanne was enjoying teaching music and drama in an international school. Her husband owned a successful restaurant. They had one delightful son, Mark Allan (Marky) who was three years old. He stayed with us while his parents were at work. They were also eagerly anticipating the birth of another child in five months.

On a trip in 1998 to see Oot's grandmother, a wheel came off of their borrowed pick-up. They slid into a light pole. The grandson, Marky, died of head injuries, and both parents were critically injured. The expected baby was lost due to the anesthetics during our daughter's extensive face surgery. Within a year, her family was shattered. They divorced and our daughter left Thailand.

How could I "take heart" or "be of good cheer" as the scripture commands? I had advised so many others before, but now I had to counsel myself.

I would like to share with you some of my struggles to come through this and declare, as Paul did in Romans 5:2-3, "We rejoice in the hope of the glory of God. Not only so, but we also rejoice in our suffering..."

How can one rejoice in suffering? It is human nature to cry out "Why? Why?" We know this is a mystery that no one has ever answered completely. Now, we can only see through the glass dimly, but we are created to reason. We cannot help trying to find the best answers to satisfy our questions.

As part of our personal relationship with God, we are allowed to struggle as Job and Habakkuk did in the Old Testament. Even Jesus called out on the cross, "My God, my God, why have you forsaken me?" It is in our nature to wrestle with this. Even though we may come away with a limp as Jacob did, we trust with Jacob that we will receive a blessing in the struggle.

Faith is not just an emotion. Faith is a decision! Are we going to trust God or not? The amazing thing is that when we do turn to the Lord and trust him, He brings good out of whatever happens to us. We ponder this promise as we wait to see what good can possibly come from suffering. There are times when it is impossible to see how anything good can come from a situation. In those times, we must decide to trust God's promise in Romans 8:28 that all things work together for good according to his purpose. We may only see the good after the resurrection.

During the time of our sorrow, we saw some of the first fruits of God's goodness in the tremendous outpouring of love in our family and from our friends. This tragedy brought a sharing of love with our family and friends at a much deeper level than ever before.

Our son-in-law, "Oot," was the first Christian in his family. His family stayed in the room the week we were in the hospital. They watched us pray and pray for healing. Still Marky died. Then, his family moved to live next door to us in our daughter's house for two weeks after the funeral.

Again and again, I had to reassure myself that God wanted to speak to them and that we should present the Gospel as best we could. I prayed for an "open door" when I might offer them the opportunity to receive Jesus. However, it seemed there was never a convenient time. Finally, the last day came, and they were packing to leave. I asked them to stop long enough to let me explain the Good news.

Overcoming my own doubts that they would respond, I asked them if they would like to pray. The oldest son immediately said yes. He told me that when they had gone to church with us the day before, the words of the hymns had so much meaning that he had chills with every song. "We felt God's presence in the hospital," he said. Then Oot's mother, his oldest brother and wife, his youngest brother, and grandmother all prayed to receive Jesus Christ.

After the prayer, I asked the grandmother where Jesus was now, and she said, "In my heart." Then she asked for a Bible so that her granddaughter could read to her when she reached her home.

After two years of depression, Oot is once more functioning. He is running a successful restaurant and playing in a church orchestra every Sunday. Our daughter has remarried and is teaching in Gabon, Africa. In September 2002, she gave birth to a baby daughter, Emma Jane.

The story is not over yet. We are trusting for God's long-term healing for us all. Now, when I sit, mostly in silence, with someone else in their grief, they know I understand.

Whatever happens, our family testifies to you that we've experienced again the deep peace and joy that come through a decision to trust in Jesus. We have been supported by the love of our family and friends. We thank God for the gift of life, whatever it brings and however long it lasts on earth. We declare with Job even, "…after my skin has been destroyed, yet in my flesh I will see God…" (Job 19:26)

Ruthanne is holding Marky (3rd from right)
with the rest of the family
(Christmas, 1996)

COME, I SHOW YOU

"Jesus said, 'Let the children come to me, and do not hinder them, for the kingdom of heaven belongs to such as these.'"
Mt. 19:14

A little while after our grandson, Marky, and our daughter's unborn child died, Joan was sitting on our upstairs veranda, very despondent. She couldn't control her grief and cried out to the Lord for comfort. She closed her eyes to try to pray. When she did, everything was black as though she had died. She opened her eyes, looked up and saw a little curly headed angel running towards her from the light of heaven. He was holding out his hand, calling, "Come, Grandma, I show you."

Then Joan remembered how Marky used to run out to meet her, holding out his hand and calling, "Come, Grandma, I show you." He wanted to show her a grasshopper or pretty bug. As her own children were growing up, there was a tendency to put them off about little things with, "Just a minute." By then the butterfly would have flown, or the grasshopper hopped. Now, with grandchildren, she was not going to miss the opportunity. She always took Marky's hand to see whatever it was he wanted to show her.

She felt that God had sent Marky to show her heaven. Before this vision, Joan said she was never ready to die. She enjoyed life too much. Now she thought, "I'm ready. I look forward to being reunited with Marky."

Joan says, "Jesus is like that. He does not leave us alone with only principles or teachings. He comes to us, takes us by the hand and says, 'Come, I'll show you – I'll show you eternal life.'"

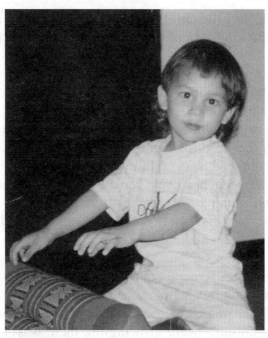

Marky pretending to play the piano (January, 1997)

We were greatly moved by the many memorial gifts, which were sent after Mark's death. We used them to develop a little park in our community. Privately, we call it, Marks Park, but have not asked for that to be the official name. The memorial gifts provided lights so the young people could play football (soccer) and volleyball at night. We offered to provide half the funds for a basketball court if the community council would provide the other half. They did and asked us to hold a worship service to dedicate the court. The youth held a footfall tournament last year and asked me to give an opening prayer and a closing speech. Recently, we received a memorial gift for young children's playground equipment. Mark's life was short, but is still shining.

CHAPTER 6

HELP ME IN MY TROUBLE

"...call upon me in the day of trouble; I will deliver you..."
Ps. 50:15

A VERY PRESENT HELP

"God is our refuge and strength, an ever present help in trouble." Ps. 46:1

The following stories are a part of my experience in facing the problem of suffering and trouble. No one can really explain suffering in a satisfactory way, nor can anyone escape it. No one comes through this life unscarred.

When we ask for help in our troubles, the trouble does not always go away, but God always gives us help to endure, to mature, and to grow from the experience. It has been said, "In time of trouble we can become bitter or better." When we turn to God we become better.

So pervading is suffering that the dominate belief where we live, states that all life is suffering. One sees this in every stage of life. A person is born in suffering, gets sick and suffers, grows old and suffers, and finally dies in suffering. Death is not the end of suffering because one is reincarnated. Everyone is caught in an endless wheel of death and rebirth. A person goes round and round in the wheel of suffering. The final goal is enlightment, which brings complete cessation of life in order to escape suffering.

One can see the truth of the statement that "All life is suffering." However, when we know God through Jesus Christ, we have a different understanding of life and of suffering. With God's presence, suffering can be transformed.

So when bad things happen to us, we can immediately hold on to the Biblical promises such as Romans 8:28, "We know that in all things God works for the good of those who love him, who have been called according to his purpose." Also in John 16:20, "... you will be sorrowful, but your sorrow will turn to joy."

ONE WHOM GOD CAN USE

"...we also rejoice in our sufferings, because we know that suffering produces perseverance; perseverance, character; and character, hope. And hope does not disappoint us, because God has poured out his love into our hearts by the Holy Spirit, whom he has given us. Rom. 5:3-5

One of the basic principles of life is that good can come through suffering. Some examples follow:

1. <u>Education</u> - In every test, students go through suffering, but joy follows when they learn they have passed.

2. <u>Sports</u> - The harder the match is fought, the greater the joy of the game.

3. <u>Character</u> - A person's reputation is developed by making the right decisions when under pressure of temptations, trials and trouble. The definition of character includes a good reputation for moral strength, honesty, integrity, uprightness, and doing what is right. The Greek word in Romans 5:4, which in English is translated as "character," is translated in the Thai New Testament as "one whom God can use." Suffering can help us become ones whom God can use.

4. <u>Freedom</u> - Freedom is very costly as evidenced by the sacrifices made in World War II. Several years ago we were very moved when we visited the Korean War Memorial in Washington D.C., while attending a reunion of my military unit. The caption on a black granite wall engraved with soldiers' faces looking straight at you is "Freedom is not Free."

5. <u>Raising children</u> - I have often watched Thai mothers taking their children to kindergarten for the first time. The child is in tears; it's all the suffering that child can bear. The mother is

crying, too. But she gradually moves away to leave her child to face the situation alone. Doesn't the mother love the child? How can she bear to let her child suffer like that? She knows that this short time of suffering will lead to something greater for her child.

Our suffering often is all we can bear at the time, but it is really only a short time in the eternal plan our Heavenly Father has for us. In Romans 8:18 we have the promise, "I consider that our present sufferings are not worth comparing with the glory that will be revealed in us."

When Jesus spoke of turning our sorrow into joy, He gave the example, "A woman giving birth to a child has pain because her time has come; but when her baby is born she forgets the anguish because of her joy that a child is born into the world. So with you: Now is your time of grief, but I will see you again and you will rejoice, and no one will take away your joy." Jn. 16:21-22

6. Love - Deep love comes through suffering. It seems to me that a mother's love is so deep because of her suffering for that child. First, she loses her figure. Then, there's morning sickness and a certain amount of fear and uncertainty all through the nine months. Finally, there is the pain of childbirth.

Suffering does not end with birth. The parents still have to wake up in the middle of the night, clean, feed, and take care of the infant. In fact, caring what happens to our children never ends. All that we give and suffer only strengthens our love for our children.

7. Meeting God - Many of us have found that suffering brings us to God. It is so easy to forget about God when everything is all right. I know more people who found the reality of God through suffering than through any other experience.

8. Salvation – Suffering brought salvation. In Hebrews 2:10 we read, "In bringing many sons to glory, it was fitting that God, for whom and through whom everything exists, should make the author of their salvation perfect through suffering."

The cross in New Testament times was a symbol of terrible agony, torture, and death. But God's love has changed the image of the cross so much that now people wear it for decoration, even sometimes when they don't know the meaning.

All over the world, the Red Cross is a symbol of caring for the needy. God has redeemed this symbol of death, and now it shows that God's love overcomes human hate; that God's goodness redeems our sin; that God's power triumphs over Satan and even over the final enemy, death.

After the loss of our grandson, long-time missionary friends, Dick and Charlotte Worley, wrote us a letter of comfort and told us this story.

In the 1873 great Chicago fire, Horatio G. Spafford lost all his property. While trying to start over again, he sent his wife and four children to Europe. Their ship was rammed on the voyage across the Atlantic. Many were lost, and his wife sent a cable saying briefly, "saved alone."

Later, he received the full message. All four of their children perished. Only his wife survived. When Spafford went to Europe to be with his wife, she told him, "We've not lost our children, we've just been separated from them for a time."

On the voyage back to America, the captain told them they were near the spot where the ship had gone down. Spafford went to his cabin and wrote the words of the hymn that Sam

Youngmi sang so movingly the night of Marky's memorial: "It is Well with My Soul."

> When peace like a river attendeth my way, When sorrows like sea billows roll; What ever my lot, thou hast taught me to say, 'It is well with my soul.'

> Though Satan should buffet, tho' trials should come, let this blest assurance control, that Christ hath regarded my helpless estate, and hath shed his own blood for my soul.

> My sin – O, the bliss of this glorious thought, My sin – not in part but the whole, Is nailed to the cross and I bear it no more, Praise the Lord, praise the Lord, O my soul.

> And Lord, haste the day when my faith shall be sight, The clouds be rolled back as a scroll, The trump shall resound and the Lord shall descend, 'even so' - It is well with my soul.

Making the decision to receive Jesus Christ as Lord of every moment of my life makes it well with my soul. For we can be sure, "...that neither death nor life, neither angels nor demons, neither the present nor the future, nor any powers, neither height nor depth, nor anything else in all creation, will be able to separate us from the love of God that is in Christ Jesus our Lord." (Rom.8:38-39)

I'VE WAITED EIGHT YEARS

"Therefore confess your sins to each other and pray for each other so that you may be healed." Jas. 5:16

"...leave your gift there in front of the altar. First go and be reconciled to your brother; then come and offer your gift." Mt. 5:24

Many of our troubles in personal and social life are due to the refusal to admit our own faults, regardless of our age. In a broken relationship, for example, the most mature Christian adult should lead the way in humility by being the first to admit his or her own wrong to the younger person. "Younger" means either younger in years of age or in faith.

It seems natural in Thai society for the younger person to ask forgiveness of the older. We older people are not expected to confess our wrongdoing. During our church planting days we were living on the Sahabamrung Academy grounds in SamYaek village. God taught me a lesson that older people should set the example in confession of wrongdoing.

Many times a young student would ask forgiveness, and we older people would magnanimously grant it. However, it was quite obvious the younger folks could see that we had our faults too. The example we were presenting taught younger students and new believers that: "As a young person you are wrong, but older adults do no wrong."

Our church congregation grew to 150 members, and we built a beautiful church. While we were planning a big dedication celebration, the generator motor broke down. It was our only power from 7:30 to 10:00 P.M. It was repaired, and I sent word, "Don't crank the motor until I check it one more time."

A few hours later I heard the diesel engine sputter to life. Angrily, I rushed over to a group of students with the demanding question, "Who started that motor?" "I did," answered Sopah, the President of the Student Body. Harshly, I asked, "Why did you do that? I said no one was to touch it!" He replied, "The head teacher told me to." What could I say? I turned and stormed away.

Fortunately, the motor worked fine and the dedication was a great success. Over 800 Christians and non-Christians marched in procession up the steps for the dedication worship ceremony. The Provincial Governor and the National Director of Religious Affairs gave encouraging speeches.

Dedication of Sam Yaek Church (January 25, 1970)

A few days later just at sundown, I was alone praying and rejoicing in the church. Sopah and another student shouted to me from outside the church, "The head teacher wants to see you." The loud manner in which they called me seemed impolite, and not at all in keeping with Thai culture.

For the next two days I questioned whether they really had been rude, or whether it was just my imagination. Then it occurred to me that blaming Sopah for starting the motor, when it wasn't his fault, might have caused their reaction.

Reluctantly, I realized that now I had to be the example of an adult confessing wrong. I called in the two boys and told them, "I have been disturbed by the disrespect you showed in the way you called out to me at the church several days ago. Then I decided you probably did it because I had unfairly blamed you about the motor." With an inner struggle, I continued, "Please forgive me." They immediately replied, "Never mind, it's all right."

I waited, expecting them to ask my forgiveness, but they said nothing. After a little silence they gave a Thai "wai" to leave. (A wai is a way of showing respect by putting both hands together.) I let them go, thinking that my idea of being an example had been a failure.

Several years passed. I knew that Sopah had graduated from a top university. He was working for a Christian hospital in central Thailand. One day as I was walking back to my home not far from the seminary where I taught, I saw Sopah walking down the same road. He said he had been to a meeting. I invited him to stop by my house, and he accepted. As we walked to the house, I remembered the time when he had not asked for forgiveness after I had done so first. I would certainly never mention it to him now.

Once inside my home, I served him a drink of cold water. When I sat down beside him on the couch he leaned over to me, put his hands together in a humble Thai "wai," and bowed down with his head on his hands in my lap. Then he said, "I have been waiting eight years to do this. When you asked us to forgive you that day in Sam Yaek, we were very pleased with ourselves. We felt we had won. The teacher apologized to us. But I could never get over knowing that we had done wrong in not asking your forgiveness too. I am so glad that now I have the opportunity to say, "I'm sorry."

Later Sopah resigned his position at the hospital, graduated from seminary, and is now a very effective missionary in a neighboring country. The seed of humble confession so reluctantly planted is still bearing fruit. Jesus often prods us saying, "The only way I can help you get rid of this trouble is for you to say, 'I'm sorry.'"

Basketball game at Sahabamrung Academy,
Sam Yaek Village (1967)

THAT PIECE OF GLASS

"And we know that in all things God works for the good of those who love him, who have been called according to his purpose." Rom. 8:28

One of the best illustrations of the truth of the above scripture is the story of the formation of the Christian Communications Institute (CCI), where we use performing arts and media to help people understand and experience the truth of Jesus in Thai culture. The Thai Folk Drama (Likay) story began one Sunday morning, in 1974, when I picked up a young student who was injured in an accident on the road south of Chiang Mai.

I was going to church to see one of my students. As I parked in front of the building, I heard a loud crash. I never got into the church. A van driven by a missionary I knew had sideswiped a bus. Two missionary children had superficial cuts on their face. A young Thai girl was holding her eye and seemed to be seriously injured. I took her to McCormick Hospital, started by the Presbyterian Mission, and sat helplessly beside her bed when she was told that a piece of glass had pierced her eye.

I prayed silently, "God, what can I say?" The answer came to me, "There is a plan." Faith is a decision, and I decided to believe that all things do work together for good for those who love the Lord. I had been on my way to church, now I was sitting in the hospital. I told her, "God has a plan for this situation," even though I could not imagine what it might be.

In the process of helping her, I learned that she came from a family of professional Likay actors and musicians. Three years earlier, Lamut, the bandit who was told about in chapter 3, had urged us to use Likay to help Thai people understand the gospel. That conversation came to mind from time to time. Now, when I learned that Kajon came from a Likay family, I remembered Lamut's words. Yet, I did not know how it could work.

One day, I told my evangelism class that we were going to visit Kajon in the hospital, present the gospel again and offer her an opportunity to pray to receive Jesus as Lord and Savior. My students protested, saying, "It is too soon. She will pray just to make you happy."

I replied, "Yes, this may be true. There is a doubt that always arises when we decide to share the truth of Jesus, but we will be offering her the very best thing we have in our lives. God has communicated throughout history, through the Bible and through our own lives. We cannot know if she is sincere or not, but our task is to give her the opportunity. If she opens her heart, we can trust God to shine in love." Kajon did pray that day.

When she returned home after being in and out of the hospital for two months, it was time to take her Government exams. She had missed so much school that she felt she had no hope of passing. One day she put a rope around her neck to kill herself. At that moment she saw a little booklet about God we had given her. She remembered that she could pray to God, and cried out, "God if you are really with me, help me pass my exams."

Receiving strength to return to her studies, Kajon took the exams and was one of ten in the class who passed. She said, "This had to be God," and started a prayer group in her class. Soon 10 of her friends also prayed to receive Christ.

She was baptized. She committed herself to serve God and study at our seminary. The seminary and the nursing school at McCormick Hospital had just merged to become what is now Payap University. After a lot of effort, the insurance company settled, with enough money to pay the hospital bills and her first year of college.

Kajon began studies at Payap, and when Christmas came she was asked to put on a Likay for fun. I didn't see it, but when I heard about it I called her in and suggested we try a Likay with a Christian message. She said that she had thought of that too.

We began to experiment with Likay in 1976, and it was received enthusiastically by the churches. Temples and government offices have sponsored performances. The Likay Troupe has performed for 27 years, and they continue to receive more invitations than they can accept.

The Troupe began with students as part of the Evangelism Drama Project at Payap. In 1981, they became professional, and the name was changed to the Christian Communications Institute. They have toured all over Thailand, and have been invited abroad many times, demonstrating how the Gospel truths are presented in the Thai context. In 1982, they received a letter of commendation from the President of the United States after performing in front of the White House.

Kajon received a Master's degree in Theology (M.Div.) and is an ordained minister. She teaches Hebrew and Greek in a Bangkok seminary. Often, I have heard her testimony saying, "I looked down on Likay because people looked down on us. I wanted to get an education and get away. Then I was in an accident, and a piece of glass pierced my eye. I decided to trust in God, and look what has happened. I have my master's degree. The Likay I despised is bringing honor to Thailand. My family has become Christian. Finally, all I can say is, 'Thank God for that piece of glass.'"

Kajon Baina testifying about that piece of glass

Somkit Buarawong, (left) Kajon's younger sister, was a leading
lady in CCI dramas for 23 years. Boonchuay Buarawong, (center)
Kajon's father, directed CCI Likays for 25 years. Kajon (right)

CHAPTER 7

O LORD, HEAL ME

"Be merciful to me, Lord, for I am faint; O Lord, heal me, for my bones are in agony." Ps. 6:2

"O Lord my God, I called to you for help and you healed me." Ps. 30:2

YOU CAN GET UP AND WALK!

"Jesus turned and saw her. 'Take heart, daughter,' he said, 'your faith has healed you.'" Mt. 9:22

"Then Peter said, '. . . what I have I give to you. In the name of Jesus Christ of Nazareth, walk.' Taking him by the right hand, he helped him up, and instantly the man's feet and ankles became strong." Acts 3:6-7

When we trained as missionaries many interpreted the above scripture to mean psychological healing. They might admit that miraculous healings happened in Biblical times, but were very unlikely for our times. Today the religious climate has changed, and people expect miracles more easily. Here is my first experience:

In 1962, we started a monthly evangelistic clinic. Dr. Chen and Dr. Chek Ling from the mission hospital in Nakhon Pathom alternated in going out with us to Pai Hu Chang, a Lao

167

Song village to give free treatment. There was no doctor for many miles, and one had to walk or drive an ox cart.

One day a man came and asked us to go to his house to examine his father who had been paralyzed and unable to get up for about six months. After the doctor finished treating the patients who were at the preaching point pavilion, we walked over to the house.

Pai Hu Chang (Elephant Ear Bamboo) Lao Song village (1963)

We climbed up the ladder steps into the house, and the doctor examined Nai Pian who was lying on the floor. Then I told him that we had come because God loved him and had sent us to help as best we could. I explained the meaning of John 3:16 "For God so loved the world that He gave his one and only Son, that whoever believes in him shall not perish but have eternal life." The man responded, "That is true, I believe it."

About that time Dr. Chek Ling got up, walked over to the ladder and began putting on his shoes. I said, "Doctor, where are you going?" He replied, "There is nothing I can do for him." If Nai Pian had not said that he believed the Gospel, I would have walked out too. I thought that my job was to preach and the doctor's job was to heal.

Nai Pian had said, "I believe." Something had to be done so I said, "Let's pray." As I prayed, I remembered the scripture, "Your faith has healed you." I said, "If you really believe, you will cut off that spirit string on your wrist." He agreed, so I picked up a pair of rusty scissors used to cut beetle nut and snipped the cord. Then, to get it out of sight, I brushed it over to fall through a crack in the bamboo floor. The Thai elder with me said later that he got ready to run. He did not know if cutting the string would cause a fight or not, but I was new and didn't know any better.

Then I stood up, held out my hand and surprised myself by saying, "Your faith has made you well. You can get up and walk in the name of Jesus Christ." Nai Pian took my hand lightly and stood up to walk. I did not have to pull him up at all. Everyone was amazed, including me.

After that, the villagers began to bring the lame and the blind. Fortunately, I came down with malaria and was away for a month. I only had enough faith for one time. Nai Pian took instruction and was baptized. He always said, "I just say 'Jesus help me' and keep on walking."

As I tried to understand what had happened, many things ran through my mind. If this was only psychological and my encouragement enabled him to walk, I could have said, "Believe me! Get up and walk!" or "Believe in the devil and get up and walk!" But I could only say "Believe in Jesus Christ." The doctor called it a miracle.

I still do not understand it completely, but I do know that the psychological and physical are inseparable. Since then I have prayed and seen many healings. Other times when there were no noticeable results immediately, some would remember that prayer long afterwards as a turning point in their recovery. For others, complete healing would have to be in heaven.

That first healing was a turning point for me in understanding New Testament times. Jesus still heals, but he does it in his time and in his way. Our task is to faithfully pray and trust God for the results.

Dr. Chen wades in the mud to hold a clinic at Pai Hu Chang. Victor McAnallen, a Disciples of Christ missionary friend based in Nakhon Pathom, came straight from teaching. Still wearing his tie, he carries the medicine on a bamboo pole.

ANOINTING WITH OIL

"Is anyone of you sick? He should call the elders of the church to pray over him and anoint him with oil in the name of the Lord. And the prayer offered in faith will make the sick person well; the Lord will raise him up. If he has sinned, he will be forgiven." Jas. 5:14-15

We had read this scripture, but our rationalistic training made us think it was appropriate for a more superstitious time. As my worldview began to change and I was open to more of the supernatural, I became more willing to try anything the Bible recommended. Rob Collins was a Presbyterian missionary pastor in Fang. His experiences were leading him to some of the same changes in worldview.

I went up to spend the weekend and share in his ministry. An elder came to see us. He showed us a lump on the side of his throat. He said the doctor told him he had to go to a larger hospital. All indications were that it was cancer. Rob and I decided to do what James said. We asked him to confess his sins and affirm his faith. Then, we took a jar of local ointment, and prayed against any magic ceremonies that may have been put into the ointment. We told him this was not a magical act. We were doing this to show our faith in God's word.

I had read of an Anglican pastor who used ointment regularly. He felt it was most effective to put oil on your finger and make a sign of the cross on the sick person's forehead. This made sense to us because there are many areas, which are not appropriate to touch. We prayed as we anointed the elder's forehead, and because we could see the lump we anointed it as well. The next day I returned to Chiang Mai.

About a month later the church invited me to come back and preach because Rob was away. Before I preached, the elder stood up and said, "A month ago Achan Eubank and Achan Rob anointed me with oil for the lump on my neck, and look! It is gone." For the next 20 years every time we met he would speak of that healing incident.

Of course, we've anointed with oil many times since then. Some people were healed, some partially healed, in some we saw no physical evidence of healing, and some died. But I never have met anyone who regretted that we prayed, or who indicated they lost faith in God because they weren't healed. All seemed to be genuinely encouraged because of the prayer, even though the affliction remained.

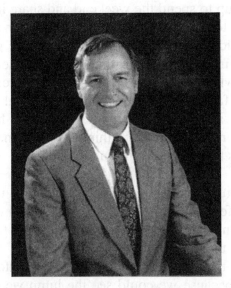

Rob Collins and I have shared many experiences
(See chap. 5 – "A Real Christian Funeral.")
He is now Director of CCI

LAYING ON HANDS

". . . they will place their hands on sick people, and they will get well." Mk. 16:18

Dr. Pradit Takerngrangsarit told me how healing became a major influence in his life. He first told me the story when he was my student in seminary. Later he sent me a tape of his sermon at his ordination service, which was a witness to the same story.

He grew up in a Chinese family living near Trang. His mother was dying of TB. Everyone had given up on her healing. Then they heard of the healing services at the Christian church in Trang, the same services referred to in chap. 3, "A Weekend with Mae Claeow."

The family was willing to try anything, so they took her to the courtyard of the church. Many people were there, and they camped on the grounds for three days.

His mother was semiconscious and didn't really understand all that was happening. Every night after the sermon the minister came, laid hands on her and prayed. At the time she didn't feel anything.

About two months after she returned home she felt much better and went for a checkup. The doctor looked at the x-rays and told her, "There is no sign of the disease. You are well!"

She believed and became a strong Christian. Her faith opened the door for her son also to believe, and they became the only Christians in the family.

Dr. Pradit received his Ph.D. in Old Testament from Melbourne College of Divinity, Melbourne, Australia, and is one of the Vice Presidents at Payap University. He still affirms his mother's healing as opening the door for him to meet and serve Christ.

Pradit and his family while he was studying for his Ph.D. in Australia. His wife, Suksiri, is in charge of Financial Aid at Payap University. She was Joan's student in music and also worked with CCI when it first began.

THE BLIND MAN SEES – Mass Meetings

"The whole town gathered at the door, and Jesus healed many who had various diseases." Mk. 1:33-34a

"When Jesus had called the Twelve together, he gave them power and authority to drive out all demons and to cure diseases, and he sent them out to preach the kingdom of God and to heal the sick." Luke 9:1-2

"Crowds gathered also from the towns around Jerusalem, bringing their sick and those tormented by evil spirits, and all of them were healed." Acts 5:16

The Bible records that Jesus healed people in the midst of crowds. The disciples also healed in crowds. Acts 5:16 states, "Crowds gathered...bringing their sick...and all of them were healed." In the present day, there is a lot of controversy among Christians about large healing meetings. It seems that there is evidence of faked healings to enhance the reputation of the healer.

Healings do take place. However, it appears that only a small percentage of those who come for healing are actually healed. There may be an objective study of this somewhere, but I have not heard of it. I speak from my experience. In general, I was skeptical.

In April of 1980, we took our Folk Drama Troupe of seminary students to Udorn in the northeast to perform in the Lao refugee camp. The local pastor, who also served as the chaplain in the camp, had invited us.

I was somewhat shocked when we arrived and were setting up, because another American came in and told me the pastor had invited him to hold healing services on these same dates.

I was very reluctant to take the chance of his services disrupting our program, and I was suspicious of anyone claiming to be a "healer." There was also a curfew which only allowed two hours to perform, and that was the length of our folk drama.

I told him we had already set our performance and asked if he could wait until early in the morning before it got hot. We would let him use our stage and sound equipment. I was very pleased when he politely said, "Yes, I am willing to do that."

We performed for several thousand refugees that night. The next morning we turned on our sound system at 7:00 a.m. for the healing service to begin while it was still cool. I climbed up in the back of our truck a little distance away to see what would happen. I wanted to see people healed, but I didn't want to be too closely identified with the meeting.

The minister announced that there would be a service on miracles. Several hundred came from their bamboo huts to listen. First, he preached a straight gospel message. At the close, he explained how to receive Jesus in their hearts and how they could be saved. He invited those who wanted to receive Jesus to follow him in a prayer.

Many people bowed their heads to pray. Then, the minister preached another sermon on the healings of Jesus from the Bible. He closed by saying:

> Jesus is the same yesterday, today, and tomorrow. Jesus healed in the Bible, Jesus is here now, and Jesus will still heal. Not all of you will be healed, but some will be.

Now, if you have asked Jesus to come into your heart, put your hand on the afflicted place and follow me in a prayer to ask Jesus to heal you. After the prayer, those of you who are healed, come up and tell us about it.

There was one man in the back of the crowd leaning on a staff, and he gave me the impression of sincerity. So I prayed, "Lord answer that man's prayers, and heal him." Afterward, the minister invited those who were healed to come forward and give testimony. Several did.

I was surprised to see the man with the staff, for whom I prayed, being helped up on the stage. The minister asked him, "What happened to you?" He said, "I don't know what happened, but I was blind and now I can see."

I waited for the man after the meeting. He had thrown away his staff and was walking with two of his friends. I asked him, "What happened to you?" He excitedly said, "I don't know what happened, but I have been blind for five years. Now, I can see. I'm going to praise Jesus the rest of my life." Then he walked away joyfully.

The minister said he had to leave the next day, and so I told him we would start the program that night 30 minutes early and give him that time for a message on healing. I emphasized he only had 30 minutes. That night the whole camp of 20,000 came to our program. People were packed as far as you could see into the dark. They knew the blind man personally, and now he could now see.

The minister gained my respect as he carefully honored his 30 minutes. He gave a brief message, prayed for the sick, and allowed a few people to testify. He left early the next morning. There was a blind man, a cripple, and a mentally ill person, all waiting for the chaplain and me when we got up. The man with the healing gift was gone. The chaplain and I prayed the best we could, but we didn't see any results. Later, that minister who led the healing meetings told us that he himself seldom saw healing when he prayed privately with people. His ministry seemed most effective when it came from the platform.

Some of the 20,000 who came to see our
Likay after the blind man was healed. (April, 1980)

I kept in touch with the chaplain for two years after that, following up on the blind man. He could still see and was praising Jesus. Then, he moved out of the camp, and I lost touch with him.

The minister of healing continued to hold mass meetings around Thailand. Because of what I had seen, together with the minister's humble sincerity, I agreed to be part of the committee when he came to Chiang Mai for 10 days of "Miracle Meetings." We were amazed when we were able to book the National

Stadium for the meetings. Christians had never been allowed to do that before.

The word gradually got out, and more and more people came. One of the missionary seminary teachers, who was somewhat skeptical as I had been, said as he watched the crowds pour in, "This must have been the way it was in the time of Jesus. People on crutches and people carried in on litters were all sitting quietly listening to the gospel sermon and the message on healing."

We brought a nurse who had been paralyzed in an accident and was unable to walk. The second night she attended, she got up and slowly walked up the stairs and on to the platform. However, when she went back home she couldn't get up again. I don't know whether there was a lack of encouragement after she got home, or whether her ability to walk was only momentary because of the mass excitement.

There were people who testified and seemed genuinely healed. However, there weren't many additions to the churches. There is the continuing problem of follow-up.

The minister held meetings in several other cities, but finally the government stopped him. I believe they stopped him because they didn't like the advertising of "miracles." There was some anti-Christian reaction, and there were also Christians who did not want to have healing meetings.

There is a division among Christians. Some are worried about what happens to the vast majority who aren't healed. Others feel that these healing meetings are worthwhile even if only a few are healed. After seeing the blind man's joy, I am inclined to support the meetings if I know the minister is sincere, honest, and resists the temptation to make a false report in order to increase his fame.

David and Dad pray for each other before going their separate
ways along the Thai-Burma border.
Photo by Thierry Falise

CHAPTER 8

WE WANT TO BE FREE

"...let justice roll on like a river, righteousness like a never-failing stream." Amos 5:24

When we feel discouraged at continued injustice and oppression, we need to remember how God has intervened throughout history.

Our family has been involved in the struggle for spiritual and political freedom for the people of Burma. A succession of brutal dictators in Burma has resulted in 54 years of civil war, religious persecution, thousands tortured and killed, and millions displaced.

The situation seems hopeless. We all kept asking, "What can we do?" In answer to this question, Dr. Saisuree Jutikul, a Christian friend who is an influential government official, suggested we start a "Global Day of Prayer for Burma." David and Karen Eubank, Joan and I, together with a few other concerned people in Chiang Mai, formed a committee called "Christians Concerned for Burma," to follow up on her suggestion. The first service was held in March, 1997. Since then, the second Sunday in March every year has been designated for the Global Day of Prayer for Burma.

The committee is calling the world to pray for justice and peace in Burma, for deliverance of the "little" people who are oppressed by military might, and for the Burmese leaders, that they will change and put their own people above themselves. In the midst of this desperate situation, we take hope in looking at what God has done throughout history. We are taking part in God's plan through the ages, which is expressed so clearly in Amos 5:24 "Let justice roll on like a river, righteousness like a never-failing stream."

We can see that this river of justice was beginning to flow in about 1300 BC when God called Moses saying, "I have indeed seen the misery of my people in Egypt. I have heard them crying out because of their slave drivers, and I am concerned about their suffering. So I have come down to rescue them..." (Ex 3:7-8a)

Around 1000 BC, Nathan confronted King David after he had sent Uriah to his death in battle, and taken Uriah's wife for himself. In 2 Sam. 12, Nathan told of the poor man who had only one sheep that he loved, and the rich man who wanted to entertain guests, but didn't want to take one of his many sheep. So he took the poor man's lamb.

David was so angry he said, "As surely as the Lord lives, the man who did this deserves to die!" Nathan replied, "You are the man.... Why did you despise the Word of God by doing what is evil in His eyes? ...Now, therefore, the sword will never depart from your house...." David did not kill the prophet.

He recognized God's truth and repented, so God continued to use him, even though the sword did come to his house. I named my son David, because King David was a leader who could admit his wrong and turn back to the ways of God.

A hundred years or so later, 1 Kings 21 tells that Queen Jezebel trumped up charges against a poor farmer named Naboth. She had him stoned so her husband, King Ahab, could get Naboth's land.

182

When Ahab went to claim the land, the prophet Elijah met him and told him, "... because you have done this terrible thing, the dogs will lick up your blood and eat your wife." And it happened. (1 Kgs. 22:37-38)

In about 750 BC, God spoke through Amos to tell the Israelites, "For three sins of Israel, even for four, I will not turn back my wrath. They sell the righteous for silver, and the needy for a pair of sandals. They trample on the heads of the poor as upon the dust of the ground and deny justice to the oppressed." (Amos 2:6-7)

In 700 BC, Micah called again, "He has showed you, O man, what is good. And what does the Lord require of you? To act justly and to love mercy and to walk humbly with your God." (Micah 6:8)

About the same time, God spoke through Isaiah:

> Woe to those who make unjust laws, to those who issue oppressive decrees, to deprive the poor of their rights and rob my oppressed people of justice, making widows their prey and robbing the fatherless.
>
> What will you do on the day of reckoning, when disaster comes from afar? To whom will you run for help? Where will you leave your riches? Nothing will remain but to cringe among the captives or fall among the slain.
> ... the Assyrian, the rod of my anger, in whose hand is the club of my wrath! I send him against a godless nation...(Is.10: 1-6)

Israel was the "godless nation," God's chosen people. Because of Israel's injustice, God raised up Assyria as an instrument for punishment.

God also promises an end to wrath for Israel and punishment for Assyria saying,

"When the Lord has finished His work against Mount Zion and Jerusalem, he will say, 'I will punish the king of Assyria for the willful pride of his heart and the haughty look in his eyes.' For he says, 'By the strength of my hand I have done this,'... Does the ax raise itself above him who swings it, or the saw boast against him who uses it?...Very soon my anger against you will end and my wrath will be directed to their destruction." (Is.10: 13, 15a, 25)

God used the Assyrians, but because they did not recognize that they were instruments of God, and did not repent, the nation of Assyria has vanished from the earth.

Around AD 30, Jesus began his ministry by reading from Isaiah 61. Luke 4:18-19 records, "The Spirit of the Lord is on me, because he has anointed me to preach good news to the poor. He has sent me to proclaim freedom for the prisoners and recovery of sight for the blind, to release the oppressed, to proclaim the year of the Lord's favor."

In Matthew 25, Jesus speaks regarding God's eternal plan for justice. He said that when the Son of Man comes to judge the nations, the judgment will be based on feeding the hungry and thirsty, taking in the stranger, clothing the naked, looking after the sick and visiting those in prison.

He will say to the sheep on his right, "Come, you who are blessed by my Father; take your inheritance, the Kingdom prepared for you since the creation of the world.... I tell you the truth, whatever you did for one of the least of these brothers of mine, you did for me." (Mt. 25: 34, 40)

About 20 years later, God sent a vision to break down Peter's prejudice against Gentiles. God led him to preach to the Italian commander saying, "I now realize how true it is that God does not show favoritism." (Acts 10:34)

Paul is inspired to expand this saying, "There is neither Jew nor Greek, slave nor free, male nor female, for you are all one in Jesus Christ." (Gal. 3:28) In God's eyes there is no favoritism among races, economic classes or sexes.

From a realistic human point of view, people are not equal. Some are weak, and some are strong; some are smart and some are slow; some are rich, and some are poor. We naturally show partiality, but God's view is different, He shows no partiality and clearly expects that humans treat everyone without partiality. When we don't, like Israel, we will have to suffer the consequences. Having to answer to God helps to keep democracy working.

We visited Athens, Greece, in May, 2002. The Greeks gave us the word "democracy." They introduced it in Athens, but it did not include women and slaves. Because there was no unifying power of the One God, their great ideal of equality could not be extended to include other cities like Sparta. Finally, internecine warfare between the city-states led to the demise of Greek power and democracy.

In the 1500s, Luther declared that every believer is a priest, and, therefore, all have equal access to God. He translated the Bible into German, so that everyone could read God's word directly without having to go through a priest.

In the 1700s, John Wesley's and George Whitefield's preaching stimulated a tremendous revival in England. This revival led to concern for the poor and oppressed. Sunday

Schools were started to teach poor children how to read and write. Debtors' prisons were eliminated.

When I first came to Thailand, an English businessman told me that corruption was brought under control in the British government because of Wesley's revival. One of Wesley's last letters was to encourage Wilburforce, who had been converted through Wesley, not to give up the fight in Parliament to outlaw slavery. Wilberforce did continue the fight, and England was the first country with slaves to outlaw slavery.

Around the time of Wesley, German Moravians sold themselves into slavery to witness to other slaves. A Moravian Bishop spoke to our mission group in Jamaica, sharing why there are so many Moravians in Jamaica. He said one day the slave owners overheard a Moravian missionary encouraging his fellow slaves from John 8:32, "Then you will know the truth, and the truth will set you free." The British slave owners were so incensed by this seditious talk that they arrested him. The jail was under repair, so they locked him up in the Anglican church.

While at Yale, I read about a New Haven minister who, before the Civil War, heard about a slave ship that had been blown off course by a storm and forced to dock at New Haven. He led his congregation to seize the ship and free the slaves. The South's refusal to free the slaves brought on the Civil War, and the United States is still paying for the sin of slavery.

One can see God's movement for freedom through missionaries like Dr. D. B. Bradley. In the mid-1800's, he performed the first modern operation in Thailand, saving the life of a Buddhist Monk. Because of this, Dr. Bradley and the Abbot of that Temple became friends. The Abbot was the prince who later became King Mongkut, and they continued to have a close relationship.

At the time of the American Civil War, Dr. Bradley started the first newspaper in Thailand and denounced the practice of Thai slavery. The King agreed with him, and wrote a letter to Abraham Lincoln, offering to send 50 elephants to help free the slaves in the U.S. He was not able to change the structure here in Thailand so quickly, but he asked his son to do it. The son, King Chulalongkhorn, did free the slaves and is considered the "Father of Modern Thailand".

In the 1840s, Karl Marx, a Jew growing up in the Christian milieu of Germany, went to England, convinced that the poor would rise up. He said that Christians only use God to keep the poor down. One example he gave in his *Das Kapital* was that Puritans went to America in the name of God and then in 1703 offered the equivalent of a $100 bounty on each Indian scalp. He thought the revolution would begin in England, but Wesley's and Whitfield's revival had already changed the social structure.

In Russia, the church aligned itself with the Tzar to keep the people subservient, and so Marx's communist doctrine prevailed.

In the early 20th Century Sun Yat-sen was converted to Christianity and led the revolution of the poor against the Emperor of China. He couldn't overcome the stranglehold of the warlords, so he turned to the communists for assistance. Even though the country became communist, Sun Yat-sen died a Christian. When our Folk Drama Troupe performed in Nanjing, we were taken up the monumental hill to his tomb. Even the communists consider him the "Father of Modern China."

As I watched Thai university students join the communists to control much of the Thai border, I realized the tremendous appeal of the communist slogan "from each according to his ability to each according to his need." This came from the influence of Acts 4:32, "No one claimed that any of his possessions was his own, but they shared everything they had." That ideal didn't last long in Acts. Human selfishness refuses to share for very long and keeps breaking down the ideals.

When I saw the appeal of communism to the poor and oppressed in Asia, I realized that this is the same as in the time of Isaiah. God used the communists, like the Assyrians, to punish injustice even though both were unjust and oppressive as well. Today we see communism fading away just as Assyria did, because the communists said, "By the strength of my hand I have done this..." (Is. 10:13)

How many people cared 100 years ago about what happened to the ethnic minorities in Burma? Today thousands of people around the world are praying for Burma. The United States and European nations, especially Scandinavia, are committed to put pressure on Burma, to help the people realize freedom and equality.

After decades under a brutal military regime, a widespread movement for democracy culminated in the massacre of thousands of demonstrators throughout the country in 1988. The military dictatorship bowed to intense pressure and held elections in 1990. The National League for Democracy (NLD) party won over 80% of the votes, and the military responded by ignoring the results of the elections and jailing many. The leader of the NLD, Aung San Suu Kyi, has been in and out of house arrest every since. To recognize her efforts for freedom and justice she was awarded the Nobel Peace Prize which also helped to bring her under international protection. The military dictatorship changed the name of Burma to Myanmar in 1989. In line with the wishes of the people in the democratic movement, we continue to refer to the country as Burma.

David's teams bring food, medicine, books, toys,
and hope to the refugees

Photo by Thierry Falise

When David visited Aung San Suu Kyi in Rangoon
several years ago while she was under house arrest, she told him,
"My favorite scripture is 'Then you will know the truth, and the
truth will set you free.' (John 8:32) The Army has power, guns,
prison and torture, but we have truth and righteousness."

In spite of the darkness and the bleakness of the situation
in Burma, we know that we are on the side of God's historical
movement. The prophecy in Revelation states that at the end of
time there will be great destruction, and it will seem as if the
devil has prevailed until Christ returns. Christians must live in
this paradox, expecting the final end, but working every moment
for truth, justice, freedom and righteousness.

The same sovereign Spirit that was in Isaiah and in Jesus
is also in us. The Lord has also anointed us to preach good news
to the poor. He has sent us to bind up the broken hearted, to

proclaim freedom for the captives, and to release prisoners from darkness. The light has shown in the darkness, and the darkness will never overcome it, whether it is in Afghanistan or Africa, Indonesia or Iraq, Chiang Mai or China, Britain or Burma.

Burmese refugees fleeing after being burned out

CHAPTER 9

MAKE US HOLY, LORD

A CALL TO HOLINESS, GODLINESS AND PURITY

"As obedient children, do not conform to the evil desires you had when you lived in ignorance. But just as he who called you is holy, so be holy in all you do; for it is written: 'Be holy, because I am Holy.'" 1 Peter 1:14-16

"Put to death, therefore, whatever belongs to your earthly nature: sexual immorality, impurity, lust, evil desires and greed, which is idolatry." Col. 3:5

"...what kind of people ought you to be? You ought to live holy and godly lives as you look forward to the day of God and speed its coming." 2 Peter 3:11-12a

"Dear friends, now we are children of God...when he appears, we shall be like him... Everyone who has this hope in him purifies himself, just as he is pure." 1 John. 3:2-3.

The death and destruction around me due to sexual behavior, and its effect on our mission compel me to write about our call by God to holiness, godliness and purity with respect to sex.

Within 200 yards of our house in the village where we live, two Christians have died of AIDS, and their wives are under threat. Down the street a Christian nurse committed suicide after discovering her HIV infection when she went for a pregnancy check. Her husband drank poison unsuccessfully a week later and then succeeded the next week. Our village headman's only son and daughter-in-law died of AIDS. The headman and his wife are raising their orphaned grandson.

CNN News reported recently that the HIV infection rate among Thai young people has risen from 11 to 17 percent. The daughter-in-law of our village pastor, who works with our church AIDS department, confirmed that report with me. The vast majority of these cases resulted from sexual promiscuity. There are 25-30 million people condemned to die of this scourge in Africa, and it is spreading around the world. The world's answer is more medicine to postpone these deaths.

We do want to extend or save their lives but, without behavioral change, those infected continue to spread this terrible disease further. Our society has accepted the pop Freudian maxim that "repression of sex causes neurosis," and has moved on to proclaim, "Everyone has a right to sex!"

In my view, it is human nature to justify what one wants to do, even if it abuses the good gifts God has given us.

Often, talk about adult sexual morality is met with the angry response, "You are being judgmental." Doesn't a man deserve some kind of judgment when he cannot control his sexual appetites, and, thus, brings home AIDS to kill his wife and children?

God gave us a blueprint of how we are to behave sexually beginning with the 10 commandments, and ending with Revelation 22:15, "Outside are …those who practice magic arts, and the sexually immoral…" Ephesians 5:3 states, "But among you there must not be even a hint of sexual immorality, or any kind of impurity..."

We have been given freedom to choose. We can live according to these commands or disregard them. We can say these scriptures are too hard and reject them, but these millions of deaths from sexually related diseases do not occur when we live in a monogamous married relationship. The wages of sin really is death. (Rom.6:23.)

We all have sinned, but we can rejoice and preach that we are redeemed through Jesus Christ. Praise God that there is forgiveness, but Jesus' message in Mark 1:15 begins with the call to repent and believe. In John 8:11, Jesus did not condemn the woman caught in adultery, but he did command, "Go now and leave your life of sin."

We cannot lower Christ's standard. Even though we fall, we must repent and press on toward the goal for which God has called us. (Phil. 3:14.) No longer do we offer our bodies to obey evil desires, but we offer them to God as instruments of righteousness leading to holiness. (Rom. 6:12-19.)

For example, if a cement contractor wants to save money in his construction by putting too much sand in the cement or too little steel, that structure will crumble and collapse. There are laws on making cement. The contractor is free to choose what he will do, but the laws of nature still take their course. God has told us in the 10 Commandments and the rest of the Bible how we are made and how best to live. We are free to ignore God's laws, but we will suffer the consequences.

The church must rise up and take a stand for abstinence, self control, and faithfulness, along with forgiveness. Christians, and especially church leaders and missionaries, must live the life and issue the call to holiness, godliness and purity.

The first expedition to the Talakone required one day by car, two days by boat, and twelve days by elephant (Nov. 1962)

Joan joined us on later expeditions

APPENDIX

Allan and Joan Eubank
Biographical Sketch

Allan and Joan served as missionaries with the Christian Church (Disciples of Christ) Mission Board in Thailand for 39 years. Although retired from the mission, they continue to serve the church as volunteers. This is their 42nd year in Thailand.

Joan Hovis Eubank grew up in Houston and Allan in Hillsboro, Texas. After his 1951 graduation from Texas A & M, in Geological Engineering, Allan served in the Korean war as a Captain in a Engineer Combat Battalion. He first met Joan in 1953 when she sang in a USO troupe for the Engineer Company he commanded. After the war, Allan worked as a geologist in Dallas and Iraan, Texas.

Joan continued her career, singing and acting in Hollywood, London and Broadway, where she received the Theatre World award as one of the ten most "Promising Personalities" of the 1957-58 Broadway season.

In January, 1959, they met again after Allan had left the oil business to study for the mission field at Brite Divinity School, Texas Christian University. Later, Allan also earned a Masters of Sacred Theology from Yale Divinity School and Joan a Masters of Theological Studies from Perkins School of Theology, Southern Methodist University.

They married in December,1959, and went to Thailand in 1961. After language study, they spent eight years in church planting and rural development among the Thai and Lao Song people in Nakhon Pathom province of Central Thailand.

During a time of drought, Joan started a handicraft industry among the Lao Song. Allan made elephant back evangelistic expeditions to the Talakone sect of the Karen tribe located on the Thai - Burma border.

They served 26 years at what is now Payap University in Chiang Mai, Northern Thailand. Allan taught New Testament and Evangelism 11 years. Two of these years, he was head of the Philosophy & Religion Dept. and the Graduate Dept. of Theology.

Joan taught voice in the Music Dept. of the University, led the seminary choir, and gave many charity concerts, including performances for the Thai royal family.

Allan founded the Christian Communications Institute (CCI) in 1981 and served as director for 14 years. Joan wrote dramas and songs and trained singers, actors, and directors. The CCI uses many art forms, both traditional and modern, to communicate the gospel in ways easily understood by the Thai people and to provide models for positive social and family life.

The CCI continues to lead more than 1000 students to Christ each year and performs evangelistic folk dramas in about 25 villages every year. The Eubanks help find financial support for CCI's very effective work.

The Eubanks have four children:

David, and his wife, Karen, serve as missionaries in Thailand, working primarily with tribal refugees from Burma. They have two daughters, Sahale and Suuzanne.

Ruthanne and her husband, James Pilton, teach in Gabon, Africa. They have a baby daughter, Emma Jane.

Laurie and her husband, Naval Commander Peter Dawson, with Sarah and David, are now based in Washington State.

Suewannee teaches high school drama in Austin, Texas.

Allan and Joan continue to serve in the Thai village church near Chiang Mai, where they live, and to do evangelism among the Wa, Karen, and Lao Song tribes. Joan is also involved with the school for the deaf and the Cheshire Home for the Disabled in Chiang Mai. At the invitation of the Nakhon Pathom Church District they return as volunteers about three months each year, in the area where they began their work in 1963.

The Eubanks intend to serve out their lives in Thailand, believing that God has called them there, and has not called them back.

CCI dancers offer a call to worship at the Eubank home
dedication - March 6, 1993. Now the house cannot be seen for
the trees.